BUDDHISM

A Religion of Infinite Compassion

The Library of Liberal Arts
OSKAR PIEST, FOUNDER

BUDDHISM

A Religion of Infinite Compassion

Selections from Buddhist Literature

Edited, with an introduction and notes, by
CLARENCE H. HAMILTON

THE BOBBS-MERRILL COMPANY, INC.
PUBLISHERS · INDIANAPOLIS · NEW YORK

COPYRIGHT © 1952
THE LIBERAL ARTS PRESS, INC.
A Division of
THE BOBBS MERRILL COMPANY, INC.
Printed in the United States of America
Library of Congress Catalog Card Number 52-1623
ISBN 0-672-60340-3 (pbk)
ISBN 0-672-51055-3
Seventh Printing

EDITORS' FOREWORD AND ACKNOWLEDGMENTS

This volume is Number One in a series entitled *"The Library of Religion,"* the aim of which is to make available to American students the most essential texts in the religious literature of the world, including in its scope the living religions and those religions which, though physically "dead," continue to have historical importance. Such a library of religious literature was planned ten years ago by the Committee on the History of Religions of the American Council of Learned Societies, and this committee has been at work ever since then, preparing anthologies which would, when published, meet the most urgent needs of students and teachers. But it was not until 1950, through the efforts of Dr. Charles E. Odegaard and a generous grant from the Edward W. Hazen Foundation, that the plans of the Committee took practical form.

The editors hope that the volumes of this series will serve substantially to meet the need of our educational institutions for readings which will give to students a direct acquaintance with the religious heritages and faiths of various peoples. At the same time, the editors believe that these volumes will appeal to a much larger reading public, since there is evidence of a growing interest in a genuine understanding of diverse religions, and a more general disposition to read in the classics of diverse bodies of sacred literature.

During these years of planning, the following men, in addition to the editors, took part in the deliberations of the A.C.L.S. Committee: Ernest C. Colwell, D. H. Daugherty, Clarence H. Hamilton, Arthur Jeffery, Carl H. Kraeling, Arthur D. Nock. Their labors were supplemented by advice and information gathered from a group of scholars too large to mention here individually; to these scholars in the field of religious studies, the editors wish to express their appreciation for generous and expert cooperation.

The editors also wish to express their indebtedness to the publisher of the series, Mr. Oskar Piest, Liberal Arts Press, Inc., not only for underwriting the series, but also for the extraordinary pains which he has taken in setting a high standard of scholarship for this series.

Special acknowledgment is also made to the following publishers for their permission to quote copyrighted material in the present volume:

American Oriental Society, New Haven, for permission to quote pp. 43-65 of *Wei Shih Er Shih Lun,* or The Treatise in Twenty Stanzas on Representation-Only, by Vasubandhu, translated by Clarence H. Hamilton from the Chinese Version of Hsüan Tsang.

Clarendon Press, London, for permission to quote pp. 106-113, 127, of *The Lotus of the Wonderful Law,* translated by W. E. Soothill.

Harvard University Press, Cambridge, for permission to quote pp. 101, 103, 105 of *Buddha's Teachings,* translated from Suttanipāta by Lord Chalmers, and

p. 73 of *Nichiren, the Buddhist Prophet,* translated by Masaharu Anesaki.

Alexander Moring, Ltd., London, for permission to quote pp. 232-233 of *Siam* by W. A. Graham.

John Murray, London, for permission to quote pp. 45-51, 54-56, 64-67, 71-74, 109-117 of *Buddhist Scriptures* by Edward J. Thomas, and

pp. 23-24 of *The Road to Nirvana,* a Selection of the Buddhist Scriptures translated from the Pāli by E. J. Thomas, and

pp. 86-87, of *Buddhist Psalms,* translated by S. Yamabe and L. Adams Beck.

Pāli Text Society, New York, for permission to quote pp. 114-117, 183-189, 308-311 of *Further Dialogues of the Buddha,* Volume I, by Lord Chalmers (translator), and

pp. 105-106, 139-140, of *The Mahāvastu,* Volume I, translated by J. J. Jones, from the Buddhist Sanskrit, "Sacred Books of the Buddhists," Vol. XVI.

Routledge and Kegan Paul, Ltd., London, for permission to quote pp. 151-152 of *Buddhist Birth Stories* by T. W. and C.A.F. Rhys Davids, and

pp. 5-6, 15-19, 94-96 of *The Life of Gotama the Buddha* by Earl Brewster, and

pp. 57-67, 64-66, 66-68 of *The Life of Buddha as Legend and History* by Edward J. Thomas, and

pp. 257-272 of *Tibetan Tales, Derived from Indian Sources*, translated by F. Anton von Schiefner and W.R.S. Ralston, New Edition by C.A.F. Rhys Davids.

Yale University Press, New Haven, for permission to quote pp. 92-94 of *Buddhist Parables,* by Eugene Watson Burlingame.

The Editorial Board
Horace L. Friess
Herbert G. May
Henry G. Russell
Francis R. Walton
Herbert W. Schneider, Chairman

CONTENTS

Preface	xi
Buddhism: A Chronology	xiv
Introduction: Buddhism. A Religion of Infinite Compassion	xv
Buddhist Literature	xxv
Divisions of the Buddhist Scriptures	xxv
How To Read Buddhist Literature	xxvii

PART ONE

PĀLI BUDDHIST LITERATURE: THE LIFE OF BUDDHA

I.	Cosmic Rejoicing at the Incarnation of Buddha	3
II.	Memories of Youth	4
III.	The Legend of the Four Signs	6
IV.	Renunciation and the Noble Quest	11
V.	Asceticism Tried and Found Wanting	14
VI.	Temptation	18
VII.	The Great Enlightenment	20
VIII.	The Chain of Causation	23
IX.	Buddha's Earliest Preaching	24
X.	The Ordination of Yasa	34
XI.	Ordination by the Threefold Refuge	38
XII.	Conversion of the Two Chief Disciples	39
XIII.	The Last Days and Death of Buddha	42

PART TWO

PĀLI BUDDHIST LITERATURE: EARLY TEACHINGS

XIV.	The Fire Discourse	49
XV.	On Bursting Bonds Asunder	50
XVI.	The Questions of Mālunkyā-putta	54
XVII.	The Questions of Vacchagotta	56
XVIII.	Consciousness a Process Only	59
XIX.	The Dhammapada	64

| XX. | The Wise Do Not Grieve | 98 |
| XXI. | The True Conquest | 100 |

PART THREE

SANSKRIT AND CHINESE BUDDHIST LITERATURE

XXII.	The Bodhisattva Ideal	107
XXIII.	In Praise of the Buddhas	109
XXIV.	Buddhist Proverbs	111
XXV.	Essence of the Wisdom Sūtra	113
XXVI.	Conclusion of the Diamond Sūtra	115
XXVII.	The Prodigal Son and the Seeking Father	117
XXVIII.	Buddha the Life-Giving Rain Cloud	122
XXIX.	The White Lotus Ode	124
XXX.	Philosophical Idealism	126
XXXI.	True Doctrine Should Stand the Test	133

PART FOUR

JAPANESE BUDDHIST LITERATURE

XXXII.	Hōnen's Quest for Salvation	139
XXXIII.	Shinran's Confession	141
XXXIV.	Hakuin's Song of Meditation	142
XXXV.	Nichiren's Vow	144
XXXVI.	The Ideal Buddhist Layman	146
XXXVII.	Philosophy of Dialectical Criticism	148

PART FIVE

TIBETAN BUDDHIST LITERATURE

| XXXVIII. | The Story of the Bodhisat Viśvantara | 159 |
| XXXIX. | Aphorisms From The Tree Of Wisdom | 172 |

APPENDIX

The Ceremony of Ordination in Modern Siam	177
Glossary	179
Bibliography	185

PREFACE

These selections from the extensive literature of Buddhism are prepared primarily as an aid to college students and readers in general who may be approaching the subject for the first time. They presuppose only elementary knowledge concerning origins and development such as may be gained from any good textbook on the religions of the world.[1] The purpose is to furnish the Western reader with sufficient original sources to acquaint him with main traditions as they are generally known in Eastern lands. Having quite another cultural heritage, the Western student requires such readings, supplementary to lecture and textbook material, in order to sense for himself the quality of persistent values cherished by Buddhists through the centuries.

Principles of Selection

As is well known, the Buddhist community arose in India in the 6th century B.C. In time it spread southward into Ceylon, Burma, Siam and Southeast Asia generally, and northward across Central Asia into China, Korea, and Japan, while directly from India it passed into Tibet in a mixed form which also became the Buddhism of Mongolia. In variant versions its literature has been preserved in the Pāli language of Ceylon, normative for Southeastern Asia, in the Sanskrit language of India, and in Chinese, Japanese, Korean and Tibetan. As full representation of all this is impracticable for a volume of first readings, limitation of materials has been necessary. Selections have been chosen from only the major collections, Pāli, Chinese, Japanese, and Tibetan, for these contain dominant tradi-

---

[1] E.g., George F. Moore, *The History of Religions* (New York: Ch. Scribner's, 1919); Carl Clemen (ed.), *Religions of the World* (New York: Harcourt, Brace and Co., 1931); Horace L. Friess and Herbert W. Schneider, *Religion in Various Cultures* (New York: Henry Holt and Co., 1932); John B. Noss, *Man's Religions* (New York: The Macmillan Co., 1949).

tions still living today. Larger space is given to Pāli literature because this includes the most easily understood versions of the life and early teachings of the founder of the faith. Sanskrit literature, except for two passages from the Mahāvastu (Nos. XXII and XXIII) and some stanzas of Nāgārjuna (No. XXXVII) has not been utilized, not only because of its more complex growth of legend and speculation, but because best portions having survival value exist also in Chinese and Japanese texts. As to Chinese literature, no attempt has been made to include examples of every phase of its vast range which reflects Indian Buddhism as well as developments in China. Only those scriptures have been selected which are most widely revered and loved by the people. From Japanese literature, four passages represent the four main sects, Jodo, Shin, Zen, and Nichiren. From Tibetan literature, which is a complex domain apart, search for elementary materials has led to choice of the famous story of the all-giving prince, Viśvaṇtara, and to selected aphorisms out of wisdom literature.

Except for one passage from the writings of Vasubandhu (No. XXX) and the stanzas from Nāgārjuna mentioned above, purely philosophical texts have been excluded. This is not because technical Buddhist philosophy is unimportant, but because it is a highly specialized field of study which would require another volume of selections to demonstrate its significance. Students particularly interested in this phase are referred to E. J. Thomas's *History of Buddhist Thought* and to A. Berriedale Keith's *Buddhist Philosophy in India and Ceylon*.[2]

With reference to translations used, while the importance of linguistic precision has been kept in mind, intelligibility for the beginner has been a necessary criterion of selection. In some instances this has meant preferring an older translation, as in the case of the Dhammapada (No. XIX). In others it has meant choosing later renderings which have greater clarity, as in Lord Chalmers' passages from Majjhima Nikāya and several translations by E. J. Thomas.

In preparing this volume the editor is responsible for the final

[2] Edward J. Thomas, *History of Buddhist Thought* (New York, 1933); and A. Berriedale Keith, *Buddhist Philosophy in India and Ceylon* (Oxford, 1923).

choice of materials included. However, he has not worked entirely alone. From the beginning he has had friendly counsel and suggestion from members of the Committee on History of Religions of the American Council of Learned Societies. Especially he would thank Professor Horace L. Friess and Professor Herbert W. Schneider of Columbia University for their unfailing interest in a project which they themselves first proposed.

For the critical reading of the entire manuscript before its final revision, a word of sincere gratitude is due to Professor Johannes Rahder of Yale University. His wide knowledge of both the scope and the languages of Buddhistic literature enabled him to make some crucial observations by which the work has benefited in its final form.

The editor wishes also to thank Professor E. C. Colwell of Emory University and Professor Arthur Nock of Harvard University for particular suggestions which have led to improvement and additions at specific points.

Since this volume contains selections from a number of works which vary in editorial style, spelling and punctuation have been revised to conform to present American usage. However, the variations in the spelling of Buddhist terms which are traditionally maintained in order to indicate the original language of the selection (e.g., Pāli or Sanskrit) have been retained where that distinction was made in the selected text.

C.H.H.

BUDDHISM: A CHRONOLOGY

B.C.
6th Century
  563 Birth of Gotama Buddha
  534 His Great Renunciation
  528 His Enlightenment
5th Century
  483 Death of Buddha: First Council at Rājagaha
4th Century
  338 Second Council at Vesālī
3rd Century
  269-237 Reign of Emperor Asoka in India
  247 Third Council at Pātaliputta
  246 Introduction of Buddhism into Ceylon
2nd Century
  Rise of Mahāyāna doctrines in India
1st Century
  Kushāna kings established in Northwest India
  100-50 School of sculpture at Gandhara and creation of the first Buddha image after the ideals of Hellenistic art.

A.D.
1st Century
  Introduction of Buddhism into China by missionaries from Central Asia, and later from India
  Beginnings of translations from Sanskrit into Chinese
2nd Century
  Philosophy of The Void systematized by Nāgārjuna in India
4th Century
  c. 300-350 Philosophical idealism developed as a system by Asanga and Vasubandhu in India
  c. 344-413 Kumārajīva, famous translator of Indian texts into Chinese
  372 Buddhism introduced into Korea from China
6th Century
  552 Official introduction of Buddhism into Japan from Korea
7th Century
  c. 630 Introduction of Buddhism into Tibet
  629-645 Hsüan Tsang traveled and studied in India. Greatest of the Chinese Buddhist pilgrim-scholars
7th-10th Centuries
  Rise of Tantric Schools and Decline of Buddhism in India
12th-14th Centuries
  Rise of the four main sects of popular Buddhism in Japan. Jodo, Shin, Zen, and Nichiren.

BUDDHISM

A Religion of Infinite Compassion

As a historical movement integral to the cultural heritage of different peoples in East Asia, Buddhism is a vast subject. Its institutions constitute one factor conditioned by other factors, social and cultural, characteristic of the several environments where it has penetrated. The whole story is long and complex. As a religion, however, Buddhism is relatively simple if we consider its basic and persistent ideals. These ideals are embodied, even if variably, in the literature represented by selections in this volume. The following brief sketch is intended to orient the reader toward them.

The Earlier Ideal in India

For the beginnings of the religion we go back to the founder, Gotama Buddha, i.e. Gotama the Enlightened, who lived approximately 563-483 B.C. Historical facts concerning his life are few, but from traditions and legends preserved in the community of his followers we know the manner of man he was. He did not belong to the Brāhman priestly class but was descended from a race of warriors. He was of the Sakya tribe whose home was in Northeast India at the foot of the Himalaya mountains. While yet a prince within his father's little kingdom he enjoyed the luxuries and privileges of one expected to become a ruler of his people. Fine garments, palaces, many servants were all his. In his twenty-ninth year his wife bore him a son. Thus legend pictures Gotama as possessing all the outer satisfactions of sense, wealth, family and high station.

Yet inwardly the prince was not at peace. He was troubled by thoughts of inevitable sufferings, hidden beneath the bright and colorful surface of life. He reflected on the impermanence of things, on the universal facts of sickness, old age and death, the pain of separation from what is loved, of loving what cannot be attained

Recognition of the misery inherent in existence was made more serious by his sharing the common Indian belief in reincarnation, the belief that life with all its suffering is continually repeated in countless rebirths. A problem posed itself: is there a way of release from suffering? By seeking, can one realize ultimate deliverance and release?

Such reflection matured in Gotama's mind a resolve. In his twenty-ninth year, the year in which his son was born, he renounced worldly life for the way of the homeless religious seeker. Leaving family and native city, he first sought instruction under two religious teachers. He learned all their wisdom but found no satisfaction in it. Next he tried fasting and other severe austerities in company with five other ascetics. Six years passed without finding either enlightenment or peace. Then he abandoned asceticism as profitless, though he still continued in his own way the religious quest.

At last one day, while seated in meditation beneath a tree, Gotama experienced the inner illumination which he sought. We are told he saw into the cause and cure of world suffering, thus becoming Buddha, the Enlightened One. Arising in the strength and joy of that experience, he went forth to spend the remaining forty-five years of his life as a wandering religious teacher. Having compassion for the many suffering in ignorance and error, he sought to share with others his way of salvation and release. Such, in brief outline, is the Buddha legend, known in all lands to which the faith has gone.

What was Buddha's discovery? It was the new insight and conviction that the root of suffering is craving, craving for sense gratifications, for existence, or for what is non-existent. Craving, he taught, is the cause of rebirths into successive lives with all their continuing ills. If suffering is truly to cease it must be by doing away with just this craving and attachment to things and conditions. The way to do that is to follow an eightfold path of right ethical conduct and mental culture through meditation.[1] By this discipline craving gradually ceases, and the joy of complete spiritual

---

[1] I.e. Right views, right intent, right speech, right conduct, right means of livelihood, right endeavor, right mindfulness, right meditation.

detachment is reached. The final end is Nirvāṇa, a transcendent state of emancipation not further describable because it is beyond anything we know in the world of existence. One who attains Nirvāṇa is nevermore reborn into this world. This is the final deliverance. It is not a state of annihilation, as one might at first be disposed to think, for Buddha is reported to have taught his disciple Vaccha that he who is released is "deep, immeasurable, hard to fathom, and like a great ocean." (Cf. Chapter XVII.)

Today, Buddha's early doctrine as reflected in the authoritative texts appears formal and scholastic. Shaped for memorizing and reciting, handed down through generations of monks in their monasteries, it has become stereotyped. However, if we think of Buddha as teaching a way to serenity and poise of spirit, liberation from all desires that bind hearts to perishing things, we are not far from the center of his meaning. His keen awareness of the universality of suffering led him to a profound understanding of the universal need for inner peace. Finding a way to the experience of inner liberation led to his unselfish life spent in compassionate ministry to that need.

As Buddha traveled and preached in towns and villages of Northern India his followers multiplied. They responded to the nobility of his personality as well as to his words of wisdom. From all classes they came to hear him. Young men of noble birth like himself joined his order of monks. To them he gave special discipline for the advanced religious life. Like him they left home and worldly life, shaved their heads, donned the yellow robe, begged for their daily food and observed times and rules for meditation. Lay folk also found guidance in his words. In gratitude they gave alms or parks or buildings for the use of the growing monastic community. To these he gave rules for humane living. They were to abstain from taking life, from drinking intoxicants, from lying, stealing, and unchastity. Nor did he forget the basic personal relationships. He enjoined mutual duties on parents and children, teachers and pupils, husband and wife, friend and friend, master and servant, laity and clergy. In Buddhist literature stories meant to illustrate the right life for laymen emphasize such virtues as kindness, temperance, consideration and affection. His followers were loyal. When Buddha died in his eightieth year he left a well-organized brotherhood of monks and a lesser order of nuns which furnished the living vehicle for the preservation and spread of his teachings through India and the Far East.

In this early Buddhism we may now indicate two fundamentally important elements. First, there is the actual teaching of Buddha concerning the way to Nirvāṇa. Second, there is the example of his life and spirit. The teaching, with its Four Noble Truths and Noble Eightfold Path (See Chapter IX), was an exacting moral and psychological self-discipline. It could be fully carried out only by those who renounced the world and entered the monastic community. A person fulfilling the requirements became a saint, an arahat, ready to enter Nirvāṇa. Such an ideal corresponds to Buddha's attainment at the time of his enlightenment.

In Buddha's later career, however, another value emerged. Moved by great pity for his suffering fellow mortals, he did not keep his attainment to himself but spent all forty-five years of his later life teaching and disclosing to them a way of release from suffering. Here was an example of profound compassion, of limitless unselfish devotion to the highest welfare of others. It gave rise to a further, more social ideal. A personality of such dimension required interpretation. In the perspective of Indian presuppositions his followers saw it as the fruit of accumulated good deeds done in previous lives before he was born as Gotama. The legend grew that aeons before, he had taken an initial vow to become enlightened for the sake of rescuing all suffering beings from the sea of sorrow. In stories of his previous existences, the *Jātakas* or Birth Stories, we are told how by marvelous heroic deeds of self-renouncing service he gradually accumulated the merit which led to complete enlightenment in his last rebirth. Thus it is understood why Buddha did not keep his supreme wisdom to himself but poured it forth like the life-giving rain from heaven on the just and unjust alike. Before he was enlightened he was a bodhisattva, i.e. one striving earnestly for enlightenment to fit himself to aid his fellow men. After his enlightenment he was Buddha, giving forth unreservedly the truth of his law. But through everything his master motive was pity, compassion, a deep sympathy for all in the world who suffer.

Historically these two influences from the founder, his teaching and his personal example, gave rise to the two main branches of Buddhism known as Hīnayāna and Mahāyāna.[2] Literally, the words Hīnayāna and Mahāyāna mean respectively Little Vehicle and Great Vehicle. They refer, however, to religious careers or ways of life. In the "little career" one pursues the arahat ideal, the way through self-purification to Nirvāṇa, which Buddha originally taught. In the "great career" one follows the broader, more social way of the bodhisattva, seeking enlightenment for the sake of others, after Buddha's example. These ideals are not necessarily mutually exclusive. Both were known and followed in India, where they arose. Both involve personal fitness for enlightenment, but the bodhisattva willingly postpones arrival at Nirvāṇa, willingly continues amid the sufferings of the world in order to bring happiness to "all the living." In Ceylon, Burma, and Siam, the way of Buddha's original teaching, including the arahat ideal, has been emphasized and set in the foreground. In China, Korea, Japan, and Tibet, Buddha's spirit and example have been exalted, and Mahāyāna scriptures set before every good Buddhist the ideal of living, first, as a merciful, self-denying bodhisattva, and ultimately, as a Buddha, a completely enlightened saviour of others.

The Later Ideal in the Far East

After Buddha's time, as followers increased, many communities were formed and changes of emphasis developed in the teaching. In the third century B.C., the religion received a strong new impetus when Emperor Asoka became an adherent and promoted its spread, not only in India, but to other countries as well. This ruler was one of India's greatest. For Buddhists in all lands he stands as a great example of a lay disciple, of one who, although living in the midst of the world's responsibilities, yet promotes Buddha's teaching and

[2] These terms were originally used by later, more liberal interpreters of Buddha's meaning and spirit to distinguish between their "greater" meanings and the conservative literalism of Buddha's earlier followers whom they regarded as having a "lesser," more selfish ideal. Today these two terms have become the recognized names for the two major branches of Buddhism.

devotes himself to good works for the sake of others. Tireless in energy, he possessed both saintly piety and practical wisdom as a monarch. While his knowledge of Buddhist teachings, which we know from his inscribed monuments, was of the Hīnayāna variety, his example and altruistic activity furthered the Mahāyāna tendency.

About the time of Asoka growing reverence for the greatness of Buddha's spirit and example began to give rise to a form of literature known as Birth Stories. This literature increased through the centuries, becoming a vehicle of popular teaching in many lands. (For a Tibetan version of a Jatāka or Birth Story see Chapter XXXVIII.) As these stories relate Buddha's generous deeds as a bodhisattva in previous existences, it was natural for the idea to arise eventually that a true follower of Buddha should imitate his example and follow his career. The full Mahāyāna ideal came to flower in a vast literature composed during the first five centuries of the Christian era. The Mahāyāna scriptures originated in India, but they found particular favor among peoples of the Far East when translated into the versions of their respective languages.

In this later literature a great extension is now noticeable in the idea of the bodhisattva. No longer is the term reserved for Buddha Sākyamuni [3] in his previous existences, as was the case in the early literature. In Mahāyāna teaching it refers to a career that is open to all his followers. No longer is the idea of a fully Enlightened One, a Buddha, limited to the few beings of such attainment mentioned in the early literature. Instead, it is conceived that in the universe there are innumerable Enlightened Ones in both terrestrial and celestial realms. Furthermore, anyone following the altruistic life of a bodhisattva may look forward to joining their number. Whether householder, merchant, artisan, king, laborer, or pariah, the way is open to all. In other words, anyone who is moved by compassion for the suffering beings in the world and who resolves to seek the wisdom of the Supreme Enlightenment for the benefit of his fellows may hope to become a beneficent Buddha himself.

The spirit of compassionate altruism in Mahāyāna Buddhism has nowhere found purer expression than in the writings of Śāntideva,

[3] I.e. Buddha, Sage of the Sākya Tribe.

a seventh century Indian poet who has been called the Thomas à Kempis of Buddhism. In some of his most impressive verses he writes: [4]

> O that I might become for all beings
> the soother of pain!
>
> O that I might be for all them that ail
> the remedy, the physician, the nurse,
> until the disappearance of illness!
>
> O that by raining down food and drink I
> might soothe the pangs of hunger
> and thirst, and that in times of famine
> I might myself become drink and food!
>
> O that I might be for the poor an inexhaustible
> treasure!
>
> All my incarnations to come, all my goods, all my merits, past and present and future, I renounce with indifference, that so the end of all beings may be attained.

Such is the character of the later ideal in Mahāyāna Buddhism. As the tradition passed from India into China, Korea, Japan, and Tibet certain changes took place. While it remained theoretically true that the way to Buddhahood is open to all, it was recognized practically that the high goal is for most persons one that is far off. Really great bodhisattvas are after all few, while the Buddhas, with the exception of Gotama, are beings in the heavens rather than on earth. The common people came to rely, not on their own efforts to achieve the perfect goal, but on the merits of these great beings whose compassion and willingness to help are conceived as boundless. Buddhas and bodhisattvas became in practice deities, with images in temples and worshipped with offering, incense, and prayer. In China the greatest bodhisattvas are Kuan-yin, the Goddess of Mercy; Wen-shu, the Lord of Wisdom; and Ti-ts'ang, who descends

---

[4] After M. Finot's rendering from Bodhicaryāvatāra. Eng. translation in René Grousset: *In the Footsteps of the Buddha,* London, 1932, p. 322.

even into hell to save suffering beings. Under other names these bodhisattvas are adored in Japan, Korea and Tibet also.

Most popular of all spiritual beings in the Far East, however, is the celestial Buddha Amitabha, who in China is known as O-mi-t'o and in Japan as Amida. His story belongs not to history but to myth, although the myth is devoutly revered. Countless aeons ago, according to the scripture, by taking on himself a great vow and devoting himself to good deeds through immeasurable periods of time, he eventually brought into existence his Pure Land in which to save all who should call upon his name in faith. This realm is situated in the Western Quarter of the universe. It combines the perfections of all other paradises and there he reigns as Lord in celestial glory. To be born there is the great longing of the Pure Land Buddhists, for whom he is the "Buddha of Infinite Light and Eternal Life." Other Buddhas are also recognized but Amitabha makes the strongest appeal to the common laity.

By way of interpretation it may be said that this Lord of the Western Heaven and the other Buddhas and great bodhisattvas are mythical embodiments in popular piety of the Mahāyāna ideal of limitless compassion and mercy for all who suffer. They are seen as the helpers and saviours from above for all whose own strength is insufficient for meeting the vicissitudes of life.

Meanwhile the more direct personal embodiment of the bodhisattva way of life is not forgotten. In China, when the ordination services are held, monks still take upon themselves the vows:

1. To lead all beings without exception to salvation.
2. To make an end of all pain and suffering.
3. To study the works of countless teachers.
4. To perfect themselves in such a way that they can attain the highest glory of the Buddhas.

A Buddhist's devotion to his fellow men entails a never ending task.

In its long history and wide spread, Buddhism has manifested itself in many forms. Its art, architecture, institutions, and practices have varied under the influences of different environments. It has developed numerous philosophies and sectarian teachings which admit of no discussion here. Through all circumstances and changes, however, the idea of Buddha's great compassion has remained a constant factor. It motivates his teaching in the Hīnayāna literature. It gives rise to an explicit ideal in the Mahāyāna writings. In popular religion it is symbolized by images in temples, images of wise and merciful Buddhas, of heroic, self-sacrificing bodhisattvas, on whose altars burn lights and incense, before whom prayers are uttered, and whose names are murmured in longing and in hope. Devout souls believe that their own deeds of charity and mercy accumulate some store of merit, after the manner of the great Buddhas and bodhisattvas. And among the learned there is awareness of the deep tradition that supreme knowledge should be for the welfare of all the living.

In Conclusion

We have seen the two major values which Buddhism as a religion has given to Asia and the world. One is the idea of personal discipline to gain freedom from craving in the ultimate tranquillity of Nirvāṇa. The other is the idea of unselfish devotion to the good of others for the sake of their deliverance from ill. Both of these stem from Buddha himself, who combined the two motives in his life. As time and the generations passed, it became clear to those who meditated on his meaning that both self-discipline and devotion to the welfare of others derive ultimately from the spirit of infinite compassion which full recognition of the universality of suffering brings. Thus in its final character Buddhism is a religion of infinite compassion.

CLARENCE H. HAMILTON

OBERLIN, OHIO,
April, 1951

BUDDHIST LITERATURE

DIVISIONS OF THE BUDDHIST SCRIPTURES

The basic scriptures of Buddhism were composed in India. They consist of a wide variety of materials, differing in importance, written over a period of about one thousand years, in the Pāli and Sanskrit languages. Later these were translated and added to in China, Tibet and Japan. Main types were as follows:

Hīnayāna, or Little Vehicle, Literature

A. The Three Baskets (Collections) of the Pāli Canon (Tipiṭaka).
  I. Basket of Discipline—Rules and precepts of the Order (Vinaya-piṭaka).
      1. Classification of offences (Suttavibhanga).
      2. Sections on regulations for monastic life (Khandakas).
          a. The great series (Mahāvagga).
          b. The lesser series (Culavagga).
  II. Basket of Discourses—Dialogues between Buddha and disciples on his teaching (Sutta-piṭaka).
      1. Division of long discourses (Dīgha-nikāya).
      2. Division of medium length discourses (Majjhima-nikāya).
      3. Division of connected discourses (Samyutta-nikāya).
      4. Division of numerically arranged discourses (Anguttara-nikāya.
      5. Division of minor discourses (Khuddaka-nikāya).
  III. Basket of doctrinal elaborations—Scholastic discussions of principles and special doctrines in seven works (Abhidhamma-piṭaka).

Transitional Literature—from Hīnayāna to Mahāyāna
[Written in pure or mixed Sanskrit]

A. Remnants of a Sanskrit Canon of a Hīnayāna school known as the Sarvāstivādins (Realists). Their teaching was eventually systematized in Vasubandhu's Abhidharma-kośa.
B. Mahāvastu (the Great Story)—A large collection of legends about Buddha's life.
C. Lalita-vistara ("Account of the sports") of Buddha. More legends.
D. Buddha-carita (Life of the Buddha)—Epic poem by Aśvaghoṣa. 2nd Cent. A.D.
E. Avadāna Literature—"Heroic deeds," told of Buddha in previous existences, and his prophecies of future careers of his disciples.

Mahāyāna, or Great Vehicle, Literature
[In pure or mixed Sanskrit]

A. Notable Mahāyāna Sūtras (Discourses).
  I. Saddharma-puṇḍarīka (Lotus of the True Doctrine).
  II. Kāraṇḍa-vyūha—Glorifies the Bodhisattva Avalokiteśvara.
  III. Sukhāvatī-vyūha—Two Sūtras, Greater and Lesser, describing the "Blessed Land" (paradise) of Buddha Amitābha.
  IV. Prajñā-paramitas (Perfection of Wisdom)—A collection of sūtras, teaching the doctrine of Emptiness (Śūnyata). These include the popular Diamond Sūtra (Vajracchedikā).
  V. Buddhāvataṃsaka (Garland of Buddha)—Chief doctrines: philosophical idealism and the interpenetration and mutual identification of all things.
  VI. Lankāvatāra (Entering into Lankā)—Chief teaching: all discriminated entities are nothing but Mind-only.
  VII. Suvarṇa-prabhāsa (Splendor of Gold—Partly philosophical and ethical, partly popular, containing magical spells.

B. Notable Mahāyāna Śāstras (Philosophical Treatises).
 I. Mādhyamika-kārikās of Nāgārjuna—Consists of 400 verses for memorizing, in 27 chapters with commentary, expounding systematically and dialectically the doctrine of "Emptiness" (Śūnyatā).
 II. Treatises expounding philosophical idealism.
   1. Mahāyāna-sūtralaṃkara, by Maitreya-nātha.
   2. Yogācāra-bhūmi-śastra, by Maitreya-nātha.
   3. Mahāyāna-samparigraha, by Asaṅga.
   4. Vijñapti-mātratā. Two treatises by Vasubandhu.
     a. Vimśatikā. Treatise in Twenty Verses.
     b. Trimśikā. Treatise in Thirty Verses.
 III. Mahāyāna-śraddhotpāda (Awakening of Faith in the Mahāyāna). Exists only in Chinese and may have been originally composed in that language.
C. Vinaya-piṭaka (Collection of Rules of the Order). The material here is of a character similar to that of the Pāli Canon above.

HOW TO READ BUDDHIST LITERATURE

For those inexperienced in this type of subject matter a few suggestions may be helpful. First, it is well to bear in mind that these readings are primarily didactic. They are not historical documents in the sense of a precise, objective recording of events. Happenings in the life of Buddha, reports of dialogues between various individuals, wise and pithy sayings, parables and stories—all these were set down long after the time of Buddha and shaped to teach his ideas as later generations came to understand them. This does not mean that these documents do not contain some very old traditions concerning original events and sayings, some of them going back to the original teacher himself. It is simply that interpretation of meanings was felt to be the great thing and deemed more important than exact chronicling of events. If myth, legend and miracle could more readily convey significance, the early teachers had no hesitation in using and repeating them. This means that an appreciative, generally reflective approach to the material will be found more rewarding than an immediate exercise of one's powers of scientific, historical criticism.

In the second place, it is well at the beginning not to attempt to pin down fixed definitions of strange words such as *dhamma, Nirvāṇa, karma,* etc. Most often these are Pāli or Sanskrit terms for which no precise Western equivalents exist. Translators allow them to stand without rendering because their meanings are generally best sensed by observing their uses in various contexts. For convenient first suggestions, however, the reader may consult the Glossary at the back of the book.

In the third place, while becoming acquainted with the content of these selections, it is well to recognize that Buddhism as a religion is primarily concerned with inner attitude and spirit. Wisdom for ethical conduct is not lacking, but considered application of principles to economic, social and political problems is undeveloped. The great sayings are addressed to man's need for some ultimate integrity and serenity beyond the reach of such crises as birth and death and the inevitable transitions of life. That there is a peace which the world can neither give nor take away is a firm conviction in the realm of Buddhistic aspiration. So also is its belief that the highest life is one of limitless losing of self in universal compassion for all who suffer. While this is not conceived according to our Jewish-Christian tradition in the West, the thoughtful reader will be able to detect points where insight rises to abiding truths common to the higher life of man.

PART ONE
PĀLI BUDDHIST LITERATURE: THE LIFE OF BUDDHA

I

COSMIC REJOICING AT THE INCARNATION OF BUDDHA

Numerous legends have gathered about the birth of Buddha.[1] These legends spring from the imagination of later piety seeking to exalt the origin of Buddhism. On the Western mind they make the impression of edifying myth or fairy tale, particularly when they are stories of Buddha's many previous incarnations aeons of mythical ages ago. As literature, however, they have their own charm. The following passage,[2] emphasizing the importance of Gotama's coming, is particularly impressive.

Now at the moment when the future Buddha made himself incarnate in his mother's womb, the constituent elements of the ten thousand world-systems at the same instant quaked and trembled and were shaken violently. The Thirty-two Good Omens also were made manifest. In the ten thousand world-systems an immeasurable light appeared. The blind received their sight, as if from very longing to behold this his glory. The deaf heard the noise. The dumb spake one with another. The crooked became straight. The lame walked. All prisoners were freed from their bonds and chains. In each hell the fire was extinguished. In the realm of the Petas hunger and thirst were allayed. The wild animals ceased to be afraid. The illness of all who were sick was allayed. All men began to speak kindly. Horses neighed, and elephants trumpeted

---

[1] Buddha's dates are 563-483 B.C. "The earliest period at which we have evidence for the existence of a body of Scriptures approximating to the present [Pāli] Canon is at the Third Council held 247 B.C., 236 years after the death of Buddha."—Edward J. Thomas: *The Life of Buddha as Legend and History*, p. xviii ff.
[2] From the Nidāna-kathā. Tr. by T. W. and C. A. F. Rhys Davids, in *Buddhist Birth Stories*, pp. 151-152.

gently. All musical instruments gave forth each its note, though none played upon them. Bracelets and other ornaments jingled of themselves. All the heavens became clear. A cool soft breeze wafted pleasantly for all. Rain fell out of due season. Water, welling up from the very earth, overflowed. The birds forsook their flight on high. The rivers stayed their waters' flow. The sea became sweet water. Everywhere its surface was covered with lotuses of every color. All flowers blossomed on land and in water. The trunks, and branches, and twigs of trees were covered with the bloom appropriate to each. On earth tree-lotuses sprang up by sevens together, breaking even through the rocks; and hanging-lotuses were born in the sky and rained down everywhere a rain of blossom. In the sky deva-music was played. The ten thousand world-systems revolved, and rushed as close together as a bunch of gathered flowers, and became as it were a woven wreath of worlds, as sweet-smelling and resplendent as a mass of garlands, or as a sacred altar decked with flowers.

II

MEMORIES OF YOUTH

Concerning the childhood and youth of Gotama, non-canonical scriptures of later tradition have preserved various stories which are doubtless attempts to fill in what is actually a blank between the events of his birth and his enlightenment. In the following passage from an earlier canonical scripture,[3] however, we have what appears to be an old, authentic tradition of his conversion. It is not improbable that in later life the teacher would have recounted something like this to his disciples.

[3] Anguttara-Nikāya, I, 145. Tr. by E. H. Brewster, in his *Life of Gotama the Buddha* (compiled exclusively from the Pāli Canon), pp. 5-6.

I was tenderly cared for, monks, supremely so, infinitely so. At my father's home lotus pools were made for me—in one place for the blue lotus flowers, in one place for white lotus flowers, and in one place for red lotus flowers—blossoming for my sake. And, monks, I used only unguents from Benares. Of Benares fabric were my three robes. Day and night a white umbrella was held over me, so that I might not be troubled by cold, heat, dust, chaff, or dew. I dwelt in three palaces, monks: in one for the cold, in one for the summer, and in one for the rainy season.

When in the palace for the rainy season, surrounded during the four months by female musicians, I did not go down from the palace.

And, monks, while in another's dwelling only a dish of red rice and rice soup would be offered to the servants and slaves, in my father's house not only rice but a dish with rice and meat was given to the servants and slaves.

Endowed, monks, with such wealth, being nurtured with such delicacy, there came this thought: Verily the unenlightened worldling himself subject to old age, without escape from old age, when he sees another grown old, is oppressed, beset and sickened. I too am subject to old age and cannot escape it. If I, who am subject to old age and without escape from it, should see another one who is grown old, and should be oppressed, beset, and sickened, it would not be well with me.

While I thought thus, monks, all pride of youth left me.

Verily the unenlightened worldling himself subject to sickness without escape from sickness, when he sees another sick, is oppressed, beset, and sickened. I too am subject to sickness and cannot escape it. If I, who am subject to sickness without escape from it, should see another one who is sick, and should be oppressed, beset, and sickened, it would not be well with me.

While I thought thus, monks, all pride in health left me.

Verily the unenlightened worldling himself subject to death without escape from it, when he sees another dead, is oppressed, beset, and sickened. I too am subject to death, and cannot escape it. If I, who am subject to death without escape from it, should see another one who is dead, and should be oppressed, beset, sickened, it would not be well with me.

While I thought thus, monks, all pride in life left me.

III

THE LEGEND OF THE FOUR SIGNS

In the preceding selection the youthful Gotama is represented as becoming aware of the transiency of existence by reflection on the inevitable facts of old age, sickness, and death. Apparently upon this basis, a legend came into being which gives dramatic emphasis to the experience. With variations it has been repeated in the Buddhist literature of many countries and found representation in their art. Here we have it from an old Pāli version.[4]

Now the young lord Gotama, when many days had passed by, bade his charioteer make ready the state carriages, saying: "Get ready the carriages, good charioteer, and let us go through the park to inspect the pleasaunce." "Yes, my lord," replied the charioteer, and harnessed the state carriages and sent word to Gotama: "The carriages are ready, my lord; do now what you deem fit." Then Gotama mounted a state carriage and drove out in state into the park.

Now the young lord saw, as he was driving to the park, an aged man as bent as a roof gable, decrepit, leaning on a staff, tottering as he walked, afflicted and long past his prime. And seeing him Gotama said: "That man, good charioteer, what has he done, that his hair is not like that of other men, nor his body?"

"He is what is called an aged man, my lord."

[4] From Dīgha Nikāya XIV. (The translation closely follows the Rhys Davids version.) In Brewster, *op. cit.*, pp. 15-19.

"But why is he called aged?"

"He is called aged, my lord, because he has not much longer to live."

"But then, good charioteer, am I too subject to old age, one who has not got past old age?"

"You, my lord, and we too, we all are of a kind to grow old; we have not got past old age."

"Why then, good charioteer, enough of the park for today. Drive me back hence to my rooms."

"Yea, my lord," answered the charioteer, and drove him back. And he, going to his rooms, sat brooding sorrowful and depressed, thinking, "Shame then verily be upon this thing called birth, since to one born old age shows itself like that!"

Thereupon the rāja sent for the charioteer and asked him: "Well, good charioteer, did the boy take pleasure in the park? Was he pleased with it?"

"No, my lord, he was not."

"What then did he see on his drive?"

(And the charioteer told the rāja all.)

Then the rāja thought thus: We must not have Gotama declining to rule. We must not have him going forth from the house into the homeless state. We must not let what the brāhman soothsayers spoke of come true.

So, that these things might not come to pass, he let the youth be still more surrounded by sensuous pleasures. And thus Gotama continued to live amidst the pleasures of sense.

Now after many days had passed by, the young lord again bade his charioteer make ready and drove forth as once before. . . .

And Gotama saw, as he was driving to the park, a sick man, suffering and very ill, fallen and weltering in his own water, by some being lifted up, by others being dressed. Seeing this, Gotama asked: "That man, good charioteer, what has he done that his eyes are not like others' eyes, nor his voice like the voice of other men?"

"He is what is called ill, my lord."

"But what is meant by ill?"

"It means, my lord, that he will hardly recover from his illness."

"But am I too, then, good charioteer, subject to fall ill; have I not got out of reach of illness?"

"You, my lord, and we too, we all are subject to fall ill; we have not got beyond the reach of illness."

"Why then, good charioteer, enough of the park for today. Drive me back hence to my rooms." "Yea, my lord," answered the charioteer, and drove him back. And he, going to his rooms, sat brooding sorrowful and depressed, thinking: Shame then verily be upon this thing called birth, since to one born decay shows itself like that, disease shows itself like that.

Thereupon the rāja sent for the charioteer and asked him: "Well, good charioteer, did the young lord take pleasure in the park and was he pleased with it?"

"No, my lord, he was not."

"What did he see then on his drive?"

(And the charioteer told the rāja all.)

Then the rāja thought thus: We must not have Gotama declining to rule; we must not have him going forth from the house to the homeless state; we must not let what the brāhman soothsayers spoke of come true.

So, that these things might not come to pass, he let the young man be still more abundantly surrounded by sensuous pleasures. And thus Gotama continued to live amidst the pleasures of sense.

Now once again, after many days . . . the young lord Gotama . . . drove forth.

And he saw, as he was driving to the park, a great concourse of people clad in garments of different colors constructing a funeral pyre. And seeing this he asked his charioteer: "Why now are all those people come together in garments of different colors, and making that pile?"

"It is because someone, my lord, has ended his days."

"Then drive the carriage close to him who has ended his days."

"Yea, my lord," answered the charioteer, and did so. And Gotama saw the corpse of him who had ended his days and asked: "What, good charioteer, is ending one's days?"

"It means, my lord, that neither mother, nor father, nor other kinsfolk will now see him, nor will he see them."

"But am I too then subject to death, have I not got beyond reach of death? Will neither the rāja, nor the rānee, nor any other of my kin see me more, or shall I again see them?"

"You, my lord, and we too, we all are subject to death; we have not passed beyond the reach of death. Neither the rāja, nor the rānee, nor any other of your kin will see you any more, nor will you see them."

"Why then, good charioteer, enough of the park for today. Drive me back hence to my rooms."

"Yea, my lord," replied the charioteer, and drove him back.

And he, going to his rooms, sat brooding sorrowful and depressed, thinking: Shame then verily be upon this thing called birth, since to one born the decay of life, since disease, since death shows itself like that!

Thereupon the rāja questioned the charioteer as before and as before let Gotama be still more surrounded by sensuous enjoyment. And thus he continued to live amidst the pleasures of sense.

Now once again, after many days . . . the lord Gotama . . . drove forth.

And he saw, as he was driving to the park, a shaven-headed man, a recluse, wearing the yellow robe. And seeing him he asked the charioteer: "That man, good charioteer, what has he done that his head is unlike other men's heads and his clothes too are unlike those of others?"

"That is what they call a recluse, because, my lord, he is one who has gone forth."

"What is that, 'to have gone forth?'"

"To have gone forth, my lord, means being thorough in the religious life, thorough in the peaceful life, thorough in good actions, thorough in meritorious conduct, thorough in harmlessness, thorough in kindness to all creatures."

"Excellent indeed, friend charioteer, is what they call a recluse, since so thorough is his conduct in all those respects, wherefore drive me up to that forthgone man."

"Yea, my lord," replied the charioteer and drove up to the recluse. Then Gotama addressed him, saying: "You, master, what have you done that your head is not as other men's heads, nor your clothes as those of other men?"

"I, my lord, am one who has gone forth."

"What, master, does that mean?"

"It means, my lord, being thorough in the religious life, thorough in the peaceful life, thorough in good actions, thorough in meritorious conduct, thorough in harmlessness, thorough in kindness to all creatures."

"Excellently indeed, master, are you said to have gone forth, since so thorough is your conduct in all those respects." Then the lord Gotama bade his charioteer, saying: "Come then, good charioteer, do you take the carriage and drive it hence back to my rooms. But I will even here cut off my hair, and don the yellow robe, and go forth from the house into the homeless state."

"Yea, my lord," replied the charioteer, and drove back. But the prince Gotama, there and then cutting off his hair and donning the yellow robe, went forth from the house into the homeless state.

Now at Kapilavatthu, the rāja's seat, a great number of persons, some eighty-four thousand souls, heard of what prince Gotama had done and thought: Surely this is no ordinary religious rule, this is no common going forth, in that prince Gotama himself has had his head shaved and has donned the yellow robe and has gone forth from the house into the homeless state. If prince Gotama has done this, why then should not we also? And they all had their heads shaved and donned the yellow robes, and in imitation of the Bodhisat they went forth from the house into the homeless state. So the Bodhisat went on his rounds through the villages, towns and cities accompanied by that multitude.

Now there arose in the mind of Gotama the Bodhisat, when he was meditating in seclusion, this thought: That indeed is not suitable for me that I should live beset. 'Twere better were I to dwell alone, far from the crowd.

So after a time he dwelt alone, away from the crowd. Those eighty-four thousand recluses went one way, and the Bodhisat went another way.

Now there arose in the mind of Gotama the Bodhisat, when he had gone to his place and was meditating in seclusion, this thought: Verily this world has fallen upon trouble—one is born, and grows old, and dies, and falls from one state, and springs up in another. And from this suffering, moreover, no one knows of any way of escape, even from decay and death. O, when shall a way of escape from this suffering be made known—from decay and from death?"

IV

RENUNCIATION AND THE NOBLE QUEST

One of the oldest accounts of Gotama's entrance upon the path of religious quest tells how he placed himself under the discipline of two teachers from whom he hoped to learn the way of the higher life. Each of these taught a system of mystical concentration or degrees of ecstatic meditation. In the following selection [5] we see him master all their instruction, but without finding the peace of mind he sought.

There are two quests, almsmen—the noble and the ignoble. First, what is the ignoble quest? Take the case of a man who, being in himself subject to rebirth, pursues what is no less subject thereto; who, being in himself subject to decay, pursues what is no less subject thereto; who, being himself subject thereto, pursues what is subject to disease, death, sorrow, and impurity. What, you ask, is subject to the round of rebirth? Why, wives and children, bondmen and bondwomen, goats and sheep, fowls and swine, elephants, cattle, horses and mares, together with gold and coins of silver. Although subjection to birth marks all these ties, yet a man, himself subject to birth, pursues these things with blind and avid appetite.

[5] From the Ariya-pariyesana Sutta, Majjhima Nikāya 26. Tr. by Lord Chalmers, in his *Further Dialogues of the Buddha*, Pt. I, pp. 114-117.

[The same applies (1), in full, to decay and impurity, and also (2) to disease, death and sorrow, with the exception of inanimate gold and coins of silver.]

Secondly, what is the Noble Quest? Take the case of a man who, being himself subject to the round of rebirth, decay, disease, death, sorrow, and impurity, sees peril in what is subject thereto and so pursues after the consummate peace of Nirvāṇa, which knows neither rebirth nor decay, neither disease nor death, neither sorrow nor impurity. This is the Noble Quest.

Yes, I myself, too, in the days before my full enlightenment, when I was but a Bodhisattva and not yet fully enlightened—I too, being subject in myself to rebirth, decay, and the rest of it, pursued what was no less subject thereto. But the thought came to me: Why do I pursue what, like myself, is subject to rebirth and the rest? Why, being myself subject thereto, should I not, with my eyes open to the perils which these things entail, pursue instead the consummate peace of Nirvāṇa, which knows neither rebirth nor decay, neither disease nor death, neither sorrow nor impurity?

There came a time when I, being quite young, with a wealth of coal-black hair untouched by gray and in all the beauty of my early prime—despite the wishes of my parents, who wept and lamented—cut off my hair and beard, donned the yellow robes and went forth from home to homelessness on pilgrimage. A pilgrim now, in search of the right, and in quest of the excellent road to peace beyond compare, I came to Ālāra Kālāma and said: It is my wish, reverend Kālāma, to lead the higher life in this your doctrine and rule. Stay with us, venerable sir, was his answer; my doctrine is such that ere long an intelligent man can for himself discern, realize, enter on, and abide in the full scope of his master's teaching. Before long, indeed very soon, I had his doctrine by heart. So far as regards mere lip recital and oral repetition, I could say off the (founder's) original message and the elders' exposition of it, and could profess, with others, that I knew and saw it to the full. Then it struck me that it was no doctrine merely accepted by him on trust that Ālāra Kālāma preached, but one which he professed to have entered on and to abide in after having discerned and realized it for himself; and assuredly he had real knowledge and vision thereof. So I went to him and asked him up to what point he had for himself discerned and realized the doctrine he had entered on and now abode in.

Up to the plane of Naught, answered he.

Hereupon I reflected that Āḷāra Kālāma was not alone in possessing faith, perseverance, mindfulness, rapt concentration, and intellectual insight; for all these were mine, too. Why, I asked myself, should not I strive to realize the doctrine which he claims to have entered on and to abide in after discerning and realizing it for himself? Before long, indeed very soon, I had discerned and realized his doctrine for myself and had entered on it and abode therein. Then I went to him and asked him whether this was the point up to which he had discerned and realized for himself the doctrine which he professed. He said, yes; and I said that I had reached the same point for myself. It is a great thing, said he, a very great thing for us, that in you, reverend sir, we find such a fellow in the higher life. That same doctrine which I for myself have discerned, realized, entered on, and profess—that have you for yourself discerned, realized, entered on and abide in; and that same doctrine which you have for yourself discerned, realized, entered on and profess—that have I for myself discerned, realized, entered on and profess. The doctrine which I know, you too know; and the doctrine which you know, I too know. As I am, so are you; and as you are, so am I. Pray, sir, let us be joint wardens of this company! In such wise did Āḷāra Kālāma, being my master, set me, his pupil, on precisely the same footing as himself and show me great worship. But, as I bethought me that his doctrine merely led to attaining the plane of Naught and not to renunciation, passionlessness, cessation, peace, discernment, enlightenment and Nirvāṇa—I was not taken with his doctrine but turned away from it to go my way.

Still in search of the right, and in quest of the excellent road to peace beyond compare, I came to Uddaka Rāmaputta and said: It is my wish, reverend sir, to lead the higher life in this your doctrine and rule. Stay with us . . . vision thereof. So I went to Uddaka Rāmaputta and asked him up to what point he had for himself discerned and realized the doctrine he had entered on and now abode in.

Up to the plane of neither perception nor non-perception, answered he.

Hereupon I reflected that Uddaka Rāmaputta was not alone in possessing faith . . . show me great worship. But, as I bethought me that his doctrine merely led to attaining the plane of neither perception nor non-perception, and not to renunciation, passionlessness, cessation, peace, discernment, enlightenment and Nirvāṇa —I was not taken with his doctrine but turned away from it to go my way.

Still in search of the right and in quest of the excellent road to peace beyond compare, I came, in the course of an alms pilgrimage through Magadha, to the camp township at Uruvelā and there took up my abode. Said I to myself on surveying the place: Truly a delightful spot, with its goodly groves and clear flowing river with *ghâts* and amenities, hard by a village for sustenance. What more for his striving can a young man need whose heart is set on striving? So there I sat me down, needing nothing further for my striving.

V

ASCETICISM TRIED AND FOUND WANTING

Disillusioned with the outcome of his experience under his first teachers, Gotama turned to the practice of an ancient form of self-discipline, long honored in India—asceticism. Tradition credits him with having undertaken some of the severest forms of self-torture, a practice he followed for six years. Once again he failed of his goal, though he gained the conviction that penance was not the way to enlightenment. A description follows.[6]

[6] From the Mahā-saccaka-sutta of the Majjhima Nikāya. Tr. by Edward J. Thomas, in his *The Life of Buddha as Legend and History*, pp. 64-66.

PĀLI LITERATURE: THE LIFE OF BUDDHA

Then striving after the good, and searching for the supreme state of peace, I gradually made my way to the Magadhas, and went to Uruvelā, the army township. There I saw a delightful spot with a pleasant grove, a river flowing delightfully with clear water and good fords, and round about a place for seeking alms. Then I thought, truly a delightful spot with a pleasant grove, a river flowing delightfully with clear water and good fords, and round about a place for seeking alms. This surely is a fit place for the striving of a highborn one intent on striving. Then I sat down there: a fit place is this for striving.

[The account of the strivings is introduced by three similes which then occurred to Gotama: That of a man trying to kindle fire by rubbing a fire-stick on wet green wood plunged in water. He can get no fire, and like him are the ascetics whose passions are not calmed. Whether they experience sudden, sharp, keen, and severe pains or not, they cannot attain knowledge and enlightenment. So it is in the second case, if a man rubs a fire-stick on wet green wood, even if it is out of the water. In the third case he takes dry wood, and can kindle fire. Even so, ascetics who are removed from passion, in whom the passions are abandoned and calmed, may possibly attain knowledge and enlightenment. The importance of this passage lies partly in its being very old, as it is found in Sanskrit works as well, but also in respect to the question whether the Buddhist method of concentration owes anything to other systems. It will be seen that Gotama is represented as beginning by adopting well known practices (E. J. Thomas):]

Then I thought, what if I now set my teeth, press my tongue to my palate, and restrain, crush, and burn out my mind with my mind. [I did so] and sweat flowed from my armpits. Just as if a strong man were to seize a weaker man by the head or shoulder . . . so did I set my teeth . . . and sweat flowed from my armpits. I undertook resolute effort, unconfused mindfulness was set up, but my body was unquiet and uncalmed, even through the painful striving that overwhelmed me. Nevertheless such painful feeling as arose did not overpower my mind.

Then I thought, what if I now practice trance without breathing. So I restrained breathing in and out from mouth and nose. And as I did so, there was a violent sound of winds issuing from my ears. Just as there is a violent sound from the blowing of a blacksmith's bellows, even so as I did so there was a violent sound. . . . Then I thought, what if I now practice trance without breathing. So I restrained breathing in and out from mouth, nose, and ears. And as I did so violent winds disturbed my head. Just as if a strong man were to crush one's head with the point of a sword, even so did violent winds disturb my head. . . .

[He practices holding his breath again three times, and the pains are as if a strap were being twisted round his head, as if a butcher were cutting his body with a sharp knife, and as if two strong men were holding a weaker one over a fire of coals.] Nevertheless such painful feeling as arose did not overpower my mind.

Some divinities seeing me then said, The ascetic Gotama is dead. Some divinities said, Not dead is the ascetic Gotama, but he is dying. Some said, Not dead is the ascetic Gotama, nor dying. The ascetic Gotama is an arahat; such is the behavior of an arahat.

Then I thought, what if I refrain altogether from food. So the divinities approached me and said, Sir, do not refrain altogether from food. If you do so, we will feed you with divine food through the pores of your hair, and with this keep you alive. Then I thought that if I were to undertake to refrain altogether from eating, and these divinities were to feed me with divine food through the pores of my hair, and with it keep me alive, this would be acting falsely on my part. So I refused, saying, no more of this.

Then I thought, what if I were to take food only in small amounts, as much as my hollowed palm would hold, juice of beans, vetches, chickpeas, or pulse. [He does so.] My body became extremely lean. Like āsītikapabba or kālāpabba plants became all my limbs through the little food. The mark of my seat was like a camel's footprint through the little food. The bones of my spine when bent and straightened were like a row of spindles through the little food. As the beams of an old shed stick out, so did my ribs stick out through the little food. And as in a deep well the deep low-lying sparkling of the waters is seen, so in my eye sockets was seen the deep low-lying sparkling of my eyes through the little food. And as a bitter gourd cut off raw is cracked and withered through wind and sun, so was the skin of my head withered through the little food. When I thought I would touch the skin of my stomach, I actually took hold of my spine, and when I thought I would touch my spine, I took hold of the skin of my stomach, so much did the skin of my stomach cling to my spine through the little food. When I thought I would ease myself, I thereupon fell prone through the little food. To relieve my body I stroked my limbs with my hand, and as I did so the decayed hairs fell from my body through the little food.

Some human beings seeing me then said, The ascetic Gotama is black. Some said, Not black is the ascetic Gotama, he is brown. Others said, Not black is the ascetic Gotama, nor brown; his skin is that of a mangura fish, so much had the pure clean color of my skin been destroyed by the little food.

Then I thought, those ascetics and brāhmins in the past, who have suffered sudden, sharp, keen, severe pains, at the most have not suffered more than this. [Similarly of those in the future and present.] But by this severe mortification I do not attain superhuman, truly noble knowledge and insight. Perhaps there is another way to enlightenment. Then I thought, now I realize that when my father the Sakyan was working, I was seated under the cool shade of a rose-apple tree, and without sensual desires, without evil ideas, I attained and abode in the first trance of joy and pleasure arising from seclusion and combined with reasoning and investigation. Perhaps this is the way to Enlightenment. Then arose in conformity with mindfulness the consciousness that this was the way to Enlightenment. Then I thought, why should I fear the happy state that is without sensual desires and without evil ideas? And I thought, I do not fear that happy state which is without sensual desires and without evil ideas.

VI

TEMPTATION

Poetic legend has pictured Gotama as being attacked in the midst of his strivings by Māra, the Evil One, and all his hosts. The tale is imaginatively elaborated in later Sanskrit and Tibetan versions. In the Pāli poem here given,[7] however, Māra is little more than a personification of such doubts and attitudes as might have turned Gotama from his high purpose.

SUTTA 2. GOTAMA'S STRUGGLE

As, purged of self by struggles stern, I sat
in Reverie beside Neráñjarā,
resolved to win by insight perfect peace,

came Māra, breathing words of ruth, to say
how lean and ill I looked, how nigh to death.

Death owns (said he) a thousand parts of thee,
and life can claim but one. Hold fast to life!
Life's best; for, living, thou'lt store merit up.

If thou wilt lead a pious life and tend
the fires of sacrifice, much merit will
accrue. By struggles what wilt thou achieve?

Rough is the road, the struggle desperate.
(Thus Māra, standing by the Buddha's side.)

To Māra's words the Lord made answer thus:
The Lord: Thou Evil One! Thou congener of sloth!

I lack no peddling rudiments like these;
no jot of suchlike "merit" profits me!
Māra should speak to those who "merit" lack.

---

[7] The Padhana-sutta from the Sutta-nipāta. Tr. by Lord Chalmers, in *Buddha's Teachings*, "Harvard Oriental Series," XXXVII, 101, 103, 105.

Seeing that faith and energy and lore
have purged all Self away, why talk of "life"?

The wind dries rivers up; shall this my blood
still course when Self is dead, when Self has gone?

While blood is drying up, the humors too
dry up; and with decay of flesh my mind
grows calmer; stronger grows its watchfulness,
its garner'd Lore, its concentration rapt.

As thus I dwell, who've braved and borne pain's worst,
my heart for pleasure feels no zest at all.
Behold then, Māra, how a man is cleansed.

Pleasures of sense compose thy foremost ranks;
dislikes thy second; thirst and hunger form
thy third array; cravings come fourth; the fifth

is sloth and torpor; sixth faintheartedness;
doubts make the seventh; th' eighth, pretense, hard heart,
and pelf, repute, the pride of place, with fame
ill-gotten, scorn of others, praise of self.

Black Māra, such is thine attacking force,
which only heroes overcome in fight,
and in their conquest find abiding Weal.

Shall I cry craven? Nay; a pest on life!
I'd sooner die than brook defeat—and live.

(Engulfed in this world's bogs, some anchorites
and brāhmins wholly sink from sight and view,
and never come to know the path saints tread.)

Seeing this host arrayed, with Māra there
riding his elephant of war, I go
to fight him. May he never beat me back!

>   Thy hosts—which neither men nor gods can rout—
>   with Lore I'll crush, as pebbles smash a bowl.
>
>   As Captain of my thoughts, with set resolve,
>   from realm to realm I'll find me followers
>
>   zealous and purged of Self, whom loyalty
>   to my commandments and their lust-free Lord,
>   shall bring where sorrows find no place at all.
>
> *Māra:*   For seven years I might keep dogging him,
>   yet with the watchful Buddha get no chance!
>
>   To see if it was soft and good to eat,
>   a crow hopped round a stone that looked like fat;
>
>   but, disappointed, flew away again.
>   —In like disgust I give up Gotama!
>
> *The Lord:* In grief, the sprite then let his lute slip down,
>   as, sick at heart, he vanished out of sight.

VII

THE GREAT ENLIGHTENMENT

Extreme asceticism having failed to bring enlightenment and peace, Gotama abandons this course to try a discipline of his own. Taking food to restore his strength, he proceeds by the more natural way of meditation to wrestle with his problem. Five fellow monks, who meanwhile had been sympathetically watching his great strivings, now depart from him in disgust. Gotama, however, finds his thoughts taking shape with unique clarity, and the sense of certainty and emancipation for which he had so long sought arising. As reflected in the Scriptures, the experience was as follows: [8]

[8] In Edward J. Thomas, *The Life of Buddha as Legend and History*, pp. 66-68.

Then I thought, it is not easy to gain that happy state while my body is so very lean. What if I now take solid food, rice, and sour milk. . . . Now at that time five monks were attending me, thinking, When the ascetic Gotama gains the doctrine, he will tell it to us. But when I took solid food, rice, and sour milk, then the five monks left me in disgust, saying, The ascetic Gotama lives in abundance; he has given up striving and has turned to a life of abundance.

Now having taken solid food and gained strength, without sensual desires, without evil ideas I attained and abode in the first trance of joy and pleasure arising from seclusion and combined with reasoning and investigation. Nevertheless such pleasant feeling as arose did not overpower my mind. With the ceasing of reasoning and investigation I attained and abode in the second trance of joy and pleasure arising from concentration, with internal serenity and fixing of the mind on one point without reasoning and investigation. With equanimity toward joy and aversion I abode mindful and conscious, and experienced bodily pleasure, what the noble ones describe as "dwelling with equanimity, mindful, and happily," and attained and abode in the third trance. Abandoning pleasure and abandoning pain, even before the disappearance of elation and depression, I attained and abode in the fourth trance, which is without pain and pleasure, and with purity of mindfulness and equanimity.

Thus with mind concentrated, purified, cleansed, spotless, with the defilements gone, supple, dexterous, firm, and impassible, I directed my mind to the knowledge of the remembrance of my former existences. I remembered many former existences, such as one birth, two births, three, four, five, ten, twenty, thirty, forty, fifty, a hundred, a thousand, a hundred thousand births; many cycles of dissolution of the universe, many cycles of its evolution, many of its dissolution and evolution; there I was of such and such a name, clan, color, livelihood, such pleasure and pain did I suffer, and such was the end of my life. Passing away thence I was born elsewhere. There too I was of such and such a name, clan, color, livelihood, such pleasure and pain did I suffer, and such was the end of my life. Passing away thence I was reborn here. Thus do I remember my many former existences with their special modes and details. This was the first knowledge that I gained in the first watch of the night. Ignorance was dispelled, knowledge arose. Darkness was dispelled, light arose. So is it with him who abides vigilant, strenuous, and resolute.

Thus with mind concentrated, purified, cleansed, spotless, with the defilements gone, supple, dexterous, firm, and impassible, I directed my mind to the passing away and rebirth of beings. With divine, purified, superhuman vision I saw beings passing away and being reborn, low and high, of good and bad color, in happy or miserable existences according to their karma. Those beings who lead evil lives in deed, word, or thought, who speak evil of the noble ones, of false views, who acquire karma through their false views, at the dissolution of the body after death are reborn in a state of misery and suffering in hell. But those beings who lead good lives in deed, word, and thought, who speak no evil of the noble ones, of right views, who acquire karma through their right views, at the dissolution of the body after death are reborn in a happy state in the world of heaven. . . . This was the second knowledge that I gained in the second watch of the night. . . .

Thus with mind concentrated, purified, cleansed, spotless, with the defilements gone, supple, dexterous, firm, and impassible, I directed my mind to the knowledge of the destruction of the āsavas. I duly realized [the truth] "this is pain," I duly realized [the truth] "this is the cause of pain," I duly realized [the truth] "this is the destruction of pain," and I duly realized [the truth] "this is the way that leads to the destruction of pain." I duly realized, "these are the āsavas" . . . "this is the cause of the āsavas" . . . "this is the destruction of the āsavas" . . . "this is the way that leads to the destruction of the āsavas." As I thus knew and thus perceived, my mind was emancipated from the āsava of sensual desire, from the āsava of desire for existence, and from the āsava of ignorance. And in me emancipated arose the knowledge of my emancipation. I realized that destroyed is rebirth, the religious life has been led, done is what was to be done, there is nought [for me] beyond this world. This was the third knowledge that I gained in the last watch of the night. Ignorance was dispelled, knowledge arose. Darkness was dispelled, light arose. So is it with him who abides vigilant, strenuous, and resolute.

VIII

THE CHAIN OF CAUSATION

A basic realization in Buddhism is that things and events arise out of causal conditions. The emergence and passing of an individual in the world was conceived in accordance with this, and attempts were made to analyze the process in detail from birth on into old age, death, and rebirth. While the earliest accounts of the Enlightenment do not contain this "chain of causation," it received in time a standard form, and later commentators pictured Buddha as meditating on it immediately after his Enlightenment, understanding the root cause of pain as ignorance and seeing in the cessation of ignorance and its effects the final cessation of pain.[9]

At that time the Lord Buddha was dwelling at Uruvelā on the banks of the Nerāñjarā, at the foot of the Bodhi-tree, just after he had attained complete Enlightenment. Now the Lord sat cross-legged at the foot of the Bodhi-tree for seven days, experiencing the bliss of Emancipation. So the Lord during the first watch of the night meditated on the Chain of Causation in direct and in reverse order: from ignorance come the aggregates [elements of the individual]; from the aggregates consciousness; from consciousness name-and-form [mind and body]; from mind and body, the six organs of sense [the five senses and mind, or the inner sense]; from the organs of sense contact; from contact feeling; from feeling craving; from craving clinging to existence; from clinging to existence the desire of becoming; from the desire of becoming rebirth; from rebirth old age and death, grief, lamenta-

[9] From Vinaya, Mahāvagga, i.I. Tr. by E. J. Thomas, in his *The Road to Nirvāna,* "Wisdom of the East Series," pp. 23-24.

tion, pain, sorrow, and despair. Such is the origin of the whole mass of suffering.

Now from the complete and trackless cessation of ignorance there is the cessation of the aggregates; from the cessation of the aggregates there is the cessation of consciousness; from the cessation of consciousness there is the cessation of mind and body; from the cessation of mind and body there is the cessation of the six senses; from the cessation of the six senses there is the cessation of contact; from the cessation of contact there is the cessation of feeling; from the cessation of feeling there is the cessation of craving; from the cessation of craving the cessation of clinging to existence; from the cessation of clinging to existence there is the cessation of the desire of becoming; from the cessation of the desire of becoming there is the cessation of rebirth; from the cessation of rebirth old age, death, grief, lamentation, pain, sorrow, and despair cease. Even so is the cessation of this entire mass of pain.

IX

BUDDHA'S EARLIEST PREACHING

Gotama has now become the Enlightened One, the Buddha. What was the new insight by which he became enlightened? Two famous discourses give the scriptural answer. One is called "The Foundation of the Kingdom of Righteousness," and the other "The Discourse on Not Having Signs of the Self." They are supposed to have been preached to the five monks who were his companions during his austerities and who now become his first disciples. Certainly these discourses contain fundamental principles of early Buddhist teaching. The first expounds Buddha's Four Noble Truths. The second introduces his concept of Selflessness, or the denial of a permanent soul.[10]

[10] From the Mahāvagga of the Vinaya Texts. In E. H. Brewster, *Life of Gotama the Buddha*, pp. 57-67.

THE FIRST SERMON AND FIRST DISCIPLES— THE ATTAINMENT OF ARAHATSHIP

Now the Blessed One thought: To whom shall I preach the Dhamma first? Who will understand this Dhamma readily?

And the Blessed One thought: There is Āḷāra Kālāma; he is clever, wise, and learned; long since has the eye of his mind been darkened by scarcely any dust. What if I were to preach the Dhamma first to Āḷāra Kālāma? He will readily understand this Dhamma.

Then an invisible deva said to the Blessed One: Āḷāra Kālāma died, lord, seven days ago. And knowledge sprang up in the Blessed One's mind that Āḷāra Kālāma had died seven days ago. And the Blessed One thought: Highly noble was Āḷāra Kālāma. If he had heard my Dhamma, he would readily have understood it.

Then the Blessed One thought: To whom shall I preach the Dhamma first? Who will understand this Dhamma readily? And the Blessed One thought: There is Uddaka Rāmaputta; he is clever, wise, and learned; long since has the eye of his mind been darkened by scarcely any dust. What if I were to preach the Dhamma first to Uddaka Rāmaputta? He will easily understand this Dhamma.

Then an invisible deva said to the Blessed One: Uddaka Rāmaputta died, Lord, yesterday evening. And knowledge arose in the Blessed One's mind that Uddaka Rāmaputta had died the previous evening. And the Blessed One thought: Highly noble was Uddaka Rāmaputta. If he had heard my Doctrine, he would readily have understood it.

Then the Blessed One thought: To whom shall I preach the Dhamma first? Who will understand this Dhamma readily? And the Blessed One thought: The five monks have done many services to me; they attended on me during the time of my ascetic discipline. What if I were to preach the Dhamma first to the five monks?

Now the Blessed One thought: Where do the five monks dwell now? And the Blessed One saw by the power of his divine, clear vision, surpassing that of men, that the five monks were living at Benares, in the deer park Isipatana. And the Blessed One, after having remained at Uruvelā as long as he thought fit, went forth to Benares.

Now Upaka, a man belonging to the Ājīvaka sect [i.e., the sect of naked ascetics], saw the Blessed One traveling on the road, between Gaya and the Bodhi-tree; and when he saw him, he said to the Blessed One: "Your countenance, friend, is serene, your complexion is pure and bright. In whose name, friend, have you retired from the world? Who is your teacher? Whose dhamma do you profess?"

When Upaka the Ājīvaka had spoken thus, the Blessed One addressed him in the following stanzas: "I have overcome all foes; I am all-wise; I am free from stains in all things; I have left everything and have obtained emancipation of craving. Having myself gained knowledge, whom should I call my master? I have no teacher; no one is equal to me; in tne world of men and of devas no being is like me. I am the Holy One in this world, I am the highest teacher, I alone am the perfectly ever Enlightened One (*sammāsambuddho*); I have gained coolness and have obtained Nibbāna. To set in motion the wheel of the Dhamma, I go to the city of tne Kāsis (Benares); I will beat the drum of the Immortal in the darkness of this world."

[Upaka replied]: "You profess then, friend, you are worthy to be Victor everlasting?"

[Buddha said]: "Like me are all Victorious Ones who have reached extinction of the cankers; I have overcome sinful states; therefore, Upaka, am I the Victorious One."

When he had spoken thus, Upaka the Ājīvaka replied: "It may be so, friend"; shook his head, took another road, and went away.

And the Blessed One, wandering from place to place, came to Benares, to the deer park Isipatana, to the place where the five monks were. And the five monks saw the Blessed One coming from afar; when they saw him, they took counsel with each other, saying: Friends, there comes the samaṇa Gotama, a man of full habit, who has wavered in his exertions, and who has turned away to luxury. Let us not salute him. nor rise from our seats when he approaches, nor take his bowl and his robe from his hands. But let us put there a seat; if he likes, let him sit down.

But when the Blessed One gradually approached near unto those five monks, the five monks kept not their agreement. They went forth to meet the Blessed One; one took his bowl and his robe, another prepared a seat, a third one brought water for the washing of the feet, a footstool, and a towel. Then the Blessed One sat down on the seat they had prepared; and when he was seated, the Blessed One washed his feet. Now they addressed the Blessed One by his name and with the appellation "Friend."

When they spoke to him thus, the Blessed One said to the five monks: "Do not address, monks, the Tathāgata by his name and with the appellation 'Friend.' The Tathāgata, monks, is the holy, perfectly ever Enlightened One. Give ear, O monks. The immortal (*amata*) has been won by me: I will teach you; to you I preach the Dhamma. Do you walk in the way I show you, and you will live ere long, even in this life, having fully known yourselves, having seen face to face that incomparable goal of the holy life, for the sake of which clansmen rightly give up the world and go forth into the houseless state."

When he had spoken thus, the five monks said to the Blessed One: "By those observances, friend Gotama, by those practices, by those austerities, you have not won to power surpassing that of men, nor to higher knowledge and vision. How will you now, living with full habit, having given up your exertions, having turned to luxury, be able to obtain power surpassing that of men, and the higher knowledge and vision?"

When they had spoken thus, the Blessed One said to the five monks: "The Tathāgata, O monks, does not live with full habit, he has not given up exertion, he has not turned to luxury. The Tathāgata, monks, is the holy, most fully Enlightened One. Give ear, O monks, the immortal has been won; I will teach you; to you I will preach the Dhamma. Do you walk in the way I show you; you will live ere long, even in this life, having fully known yourselves, having seen face to face that incomparable goal of the holy life, for the sake of which clansmen rightly give up the world and go forth into the houseless state."

... [The five monks repeat twice the same remonstrances, to which the Blessed One makes the same replies.]

When they had spoken thus, the Blessed One said to the five monks: "Do you admit, monks, that I have never spoken to you in this way before this day?"

"You have never spoken so, lord."

"The Tathāgata, monks, is the holy, fully Enlightened One. Give ear, O monks . . . [as above].

And the Blessed One was able to convince the five monks; and the five monks again listened willingly to the Blessed One; they gave ear and fixed their mind on the knowledge [imparted to them].

The Buddha's First Sermon, Known as the Foundation of the Kingdom of Righteousness or the Setting in Motion of the Wheel of the Dhamma

The Mahāvagga continues:

And the Blessed One thus addressed the five monks: There are two extremes, monks, which he who has given up the world ought to avoid.

What are these two extremes? A life given to pleasures, devoted to pleasures and lusts—this is degrading, sensual, vulgar, ignoble, and profitless.

And a life given to mortifications—this is painful, ignoble, and profitless.

By avoiding these two extremes, monks, the Tathāgata has gained the knowledge of the Middle Path which leads to insight, which leads to wisdom, which conduces to calm, to knowledge, to Sambodhi (Supreme Enlightenment), to Nibbāna.

Which, monks, is this Middle Path the knowledge of which the Tathāgata has gained, which leads to insight, which leads to wisdom, which conduces to calm, to knowledge, to Sambodhi, to Nibbāna?

It is the Noble Eightfold Path, namely: right views, right intent, right speech, right conduct, right means of livelihood, right endeavor, right mindfulness, right meditation.

This, monks, is the Middle Path the knowledge of which the Tathāgata has gained, which leads to insight, which leads to wisdom, which conduces to calm, to knowledge, to perfect enlightenment, to Nibbāna.

This, monks, is the Noble Truth of Suffering: birth is suffering; decay is suffering; illness is suffering; death is suffering; presence of objects we hate is suffering; separation from objects we love is suffering; not to obtain what we desire is suffering.

In brief, the five aggregates which spring from grasping, they are painful.

This, monks, is the Noble Truth concerning the Origin of Suffering: verily, it originates in that craving which causes the renewal of becomings, is accompanied by sensual delight, and seeks satisfaction now here, now there; that is to say, craving for pleasures, craving for becoming, craving for not becoming.

This, monks, is the Noble Truth concerning the Cessation of Suffering: verily, it is passionlessness, cessation without remainder of this very craving; the laying aside of, the giving up, the being free from, the harboring no longer of, this craving.

This, monks, is the Noble Truth concerning the Path which leads to the Cessation of Suffering: verily, it is this Noble Eightfold Path, that is to say, right views, right intent, right speech, right conduct, right means of livelihood, right endeavor, right mindfulness, and right meditation.

This is the Noble Truth concerning Suffering. Thus, monks, in things which formerly had not been heard of have I obtained insight, knowledge, understanding, wisdom, intuition. This Noble Truth concerning Suffering must be understood. Thus, monks, in things which formerly had not been heard of have I obtained insight, knowledge, understanding, wisdom, and intuition. This Noble Truth concerning Suffering I have understood. Thus, monks, in things which formerly had not been heard of have I obtained insight, knowledge, understanding, wisdom, and intuition.

This is the Noble Truth concerning the Origin of Suffering. Thus, monks, in things which had formerly not been heard of have I obtained insight, knowledge, understanding, wisdom, intuition. This Noble Truth concerning the Cause of Suffering must be abandoned . . . has been abandoned by me. Thus, monks, in things which formerly had not been heard of have I obtained knowledge, understanding, wisdom, and intuition.

This is the Noble Truth concerning the Cessation of Suffering. Thus, monks, in things which formerly had not been heard of have I obtained insight, knowledge, understanding, wisdom, intuition.

This Noble Truth concerning the Cessation of Suffering must be seen face to face . . . has been seen by me face to face. Thus, monks, in things which formerly had not been heard of have I obtained insight, knowledge, understanding, wisdom, intuition.

This is the Noble Truth concerning the Path which leads to the Cessation of Suffering. Thus, monks, in things which formerly had not been heard of have I obtained insight, knowledge, understanding, wisdom, intuition. This Noble Truth concerning the Path which leads to the Cessation of Suffering must be realized . . . has been realized by me. Thus, monks, in things which formerly had not been heard of have I obtained insight, knowledge, understanding, wisdom, intuition.

As long, monks, as I did not possess with perfect purity this true knowledge and insight into these Four Noble Truths, with its three modifications and its twelve constituent parts, so long, monks, I knew that I had not yet obtained the highest absolute enlightenment in the world of men and gods, in Māra's and in Brahma's world, among all beings, samaṇas, and brāhmans, gods and men.

But since I possessed, monks, with perfect purity this true knowledge and insight into these Four Noble Truths, with its three modifications and its twelve constituent parts, then I knew, monks, that I had obtained the highest, universal enlightenment in the world of men and gods. . . . [etc., as above].

And this knowledge and insight arose in my mind: The emancipation of my mind cannot be shaken; this is my last birth; now shall I not be born again.

Thus the Blessed One spoke. The five monks were delighted, and they rejoiced at the words of the Blessed One. And when this exposition was propounded, the venerable Kondañña obtained the pure and spotless Dhamma-eye [that is to say, the following knowledge]: "Whatsoever is an arising thing, all that is a ceasing thing."

And as the Blessed One had set going the wheel of the Dhamma, the earth-inhabiting devas shouted: "Truly the Blessed One has set going at Benares, in the deer park Isipatana, the wheel of the Dhamma, which may be opposed neither by a samaṇa, nor by a brāhman, neither by a deva, nor by Māra, nor by Brahma, nor by any being in the world."

Hearing the shout of the earth-inhabiting devas, the four firmament-devas shouted . . . [etc., as above]. Hearing their shout, the Tāvatiṃsa devas, . . . the Yāma devas, . . . the Tusita devas, . . . the Nimmānarati devas, . . . the Paranimmitavasavatti devas, . . . the Brahma-world devas shouted: "Truly the Blessed One has set going at Benares, in the deer park Isipatana, the wheel of the Dhamma, which may be opposed neither by a samaṇa, nor by a brāhman, neither by a deva, nor by Māra, nor by Brahma, nor by any being in the world."

Thus in that moment, in that instant, in that second the shout reached the Brahma world; and this whole system of ten thousand worlds quaked, was shaken, and trembled; and an infinite, mighty light was seen through the world, which surpassed the light that can be produced by the divine power of the devas.

And the Blessed One pronounced this solemn utterance: "Truly Kondañña has perceived it (*aññāsi*), truly Kondañña has perceived it." Hence the venerable Kondañña received the name Aññātakondañña (Kondañña who has perceived the Doctrine).

And the venerable Aññātakondañña, having seen the Dhamma, having mastered the Dhamma, having understood the Dhamma, having penetrated the Dhamma, having overcome uncertainty, having dispelled all doubts, having gained full knowledge, dependent on nobody else for knowledge of the Doctrine of the Teacher, thus spoke to the Blessed One: "Lord, let me become a recluse under the Blessed One, let me receive ordination." "Come, monk," said the Blessed One, "well taught is the Dhamma; lead a holy life for the sake of the complete ending of suffering."

Thus this venerable person received ordination.

And the Blessed One administered to the other monks exhortation and instruction by discourses relating to the Dhamma. And the venerable Vappa and the venerable Bhaddiya, when they received from the Blessed One such exhortation and instruction by discourses relating to the Dhamma, obtained the pure and spotless Dhamma-eye [that is to say, the following knowledge]: "Whatsoever is a beginning thing, all that is an ending thing."

And having seen the Dhamma, having mastered the Dhamma, having understood the Dhamma, having penetrated the Dhamma, having overcome uncertainty, having dispelled all doubts, having won confidence, dependent on nobody else for knowledge of the religion of the Teacher, they thus spoke to the Blessed One: "Lord, let us become a recluse under the Blessed One and receive ordination."

"Come, monks," said the Blessed One, "well taught is the Dhamma; lead a holy life for the sake of the complete ending of Ill." Thus these venerable persons received ordination.

And the Blessed One, living on what the monks brought him, administered to the other monks exhortation and instruction by discourses relating to the Dhamma; in this way the six persons lived on what the three monks brought home from their alms.

And the venerable Mahānāma and the venerable Assaji, when they received from the Blessed One such exhortation and instruction by discourses relating to the Dhamma, obtained the pure and spotless Dhamma-eye [that is to say, the following knowledge]: "Whatsoever is a beginning thing, all that is an ending thing."

And having seen the Dhamma, having mastered the Dhamma, having understood the Dhamma, having penetrated the Dhamma, having overcome uncertainty, having dispelled all doubts, having gained full knowledge, dependent on nobody else for knowledge of the Doctrine of the Teacher, they thus spoke to the Blessed One: "Lord, let us become a recluse under the Blessed One and receive ordination."

"Come, monks," said the Blessed One, "well taught is the Dhamma; lead a holy life for the sake of the complete ending of Ill." Thus these venerable persons received ordination.

Anattalakkhaṇa Sutta or Discourse on Not Having Signs of the Self.

And the Blessed One spoke thus to the five bhikkus: The body (*rūpa*), monks, is not the self. If the body, monks, were the self, the body would not be subject to disease, and we should be able to say: Let my body be such and such a one, let my body not be such and such a one. But since the body, monks, is not the self, therefore the body is subject to disease, and we are not able to say, Let my body be such and such a one, let my body not be such and such a one.

Sensation (*vedanā*), monks, is not the self . . . [as above]; perception (*saññā*) is not the self . . . synergies (*sankhāra's*) are not the self . . . consciousness (*viññāṇa*) is not the self . . . [as above].

> Now what do you think, monks, is the body permanent or perishable?
>
> It is perishable, Lord.
>
> And that which is perishable, does that cause pain or joy?
>
> It causes pain, Lord.
>
> And that which is perishable, painful, subject to change, is it possible to regard that in this way? This is mine, this am I, this is myself?
>
> That is impossible, Lord.

[Here follows the same dialogue regarding sensation, perception, synergies, and consciousness]. . . .

Therefore, monks, whatever body has been, will be, and is now, belonging or not belonging to sentient beings, gross or subtle, inferior or superior, distant or near, all that body is not mine, is not me, is not my self; thus it should be considered by right knowledge according to the truth.

[The same is stated of sensation, perception, synergies and consciousness.]

Considering this, monks, the wise and noble disciple turns away from the body, turns away from sensation, turns away from perception, turns away from the synergies, turns away from body and mind.

Turning away he loses passion, losing passion he is liberated, in being liberated the knowledge comes to him: "I am liberated," and he knows rebirth is exhausted, the holy life is completed, duty is fulfilled; there is no more living in these conditions.

Thus the Blessed One spoke. The five monks were delighted and rejoiced at the words of the Blessed One. And when this exposition had been propounded, the minds of the five monks became free from attachment to the world, and were released from the cankers.

At that time there were six arahats (persons who had reached absolute holiness) in the world.

X

THE ORDINATION OF YASA

The story of the noble youth named Yasa is told in the Scriptures [11] in order to emphasize the early origin of the ceremony of ordination. It is noteworthy also for the simplicity with which it states the Buddha's teaching in approaching the laity.

At that time there was in Benares a noble youth named Yasa, son of a guild master, and delicately nurtured. He had three palaces—one for winter, one for summer, and one for the season of rains. He spent four months in the palace of the rainy season, surrounded by music girls, and did not leave the palace. Now, Yasa, the noble youth, thus attended, endowed with and possessed of the five passions of sense, once fell asleep sooner than usual and afterward his attendants also fell asleep. All the night an oil lamp was burning. Yasa, the noble youth, woke sooner than usual and saw his attendants sleeping, a lute in the arms of one, a tambour

[11] From the Mahāvagga of the Vinaya Texts, in Edward J. Thomas, *Buddhist Scriptures*, pp. 45-51.

on the neck of another, a drum in the arms of another, one with disheveled hair, another with driveling mouth and muttering. It was like a cemetery around him. As he saw this, the evils of life became clear to him, and his mind became set with aversion. So Yasa, the noble youth, made this solemn utterance: "How oppressive it is, how afflicting it is!" Then Yasa, the noble youth, put on his gilt shoes and went to the door of the house. Superhuman beings opened the gate, saying, Let no one put an obstacle before Yasa, the noble youth, in his going forth from the house to a houseless life.

And Yasa, the noble youth, went to Isipatana, the deer park. At that time the Lord had arisen at night, as it was dawning, and was walking in the open air. The Lord saw Yasa, the noble youth, as he was coming from afar, and on seeing him came down from where he was walking, and sat down on the seat prepared for him. Yasa, the noble youth, on drawing near the Lord made this solemn utterance: "How oppressive it is, how afflicting it is!" And the Lord said to Yasa, the noble youth, "This, Yasa, is not oppressive, this is not afflicting. Come, Yasa, sit down, I will teach you the Doctrine." Then Yasa, the noble youth, at these words, "This is not oppressive, this is not afflicting," was elated and glad, and taking off his gilt shoes approached the Lord and, having saluted him, sat down at one side. As he was seated at one side, the Lord gave him a due exposition of this kind: He preached a discourse of almsgiving, of the commandments, of heaven, the misery, worthlessness, and impurity of lusts, and the blessing of renunciation. When the Lord saw that the mind of Yasa, the noble youth, was prepared, susceptible, free from obstacles, elated, and happy, then he preached a most excellent discourse of the Doctrine of the Buddhas: suffering, the cause (of suffering), the destruction (of suffering), and the path. And as a clean cloth free from stain duly takes the dye, so in Yasa, the noble youth, as he sat there, arose the pure, unstained insight into the Doctrine—that everything subject to birth is subject to destruction.

Now the mother of Yasa, the noble youth, went up to the palace, and not seeing him went to the guild master, the householder, and approached him and said, "Your son Yasa, householder, is not to be seen." Then the guild master, the householder, sent out messengers on horseback in four directions, and he himself went to Isipatana, the deer park. The guild master, the householder, saw the footprints of the gilt shoes, and seeing them he followed their traces. Now the Lord saw the guild master, the householder, approaching, and as he saw him he thought, What if I were to effect such an exercise of miraculous power that the guild master, the householder, sitting here should not see Yasa, the noble youth, sitting here. So the Lord effected such an exercise of miraculous power. Then the guild master, the householder, approached the Lord, and having approached said, "Perhaps the reverend Lord has seen Yasa, the noble youth." "Well, householder, sit down, perhaps sitting here you can see Yasa, the noble youth, sitting here." The guild master, the householder, thought, Surely, sitting here I shall see Yasa, the noble youth, sitting here, and glad and elated he saluted the Lord and sat on one side.

As the guild master, the householder, was seated on one side, the Lord gave him a due exposition of this kind: He preached a discourse of alms-giving, of the commandments, of heaven, the misery, worthlessness, and impurity of lusts, and the blessing of renunciation. Then the guild master, the householder, having seen, attained, mastered, and penetrated the Doctrine, with his doubts overcome, his uncertainties dispelled, having obtained clearness of mind, dependent on no one else for the teaching of the Master, said to the Lord: "Wonderful, reverend sir, wonderful, reverend sir, it is as if, reverend sir, one were setting up what was overturned, or revealing what was hidden, or showing the way to one who was lost, or putting a lamp in the darkness; those with eyes see visible things—even so has the Lord preached the Doctrine in many ways. Reverend sir, I go to the Lord as a refuge, and to the Doctrine, and to the assembly of brethren. May the Lord take me as a lay disciple from this day forth, while my life lasts, who have come to him for refuge." He was the first in the world who became a disciple effected by the triple utterance.

Then Yasa, the noble youth, as the Doctrine was being taught to his father, contemplated the stage of knowledge thus perceived and thus understood, and his mind became freed from attachment to the passions. And the Lord thought, Yasa, the noble youth, as the Doctrine was being taught to his father, has been contemplating the stage of knowledge thus perceived and thus understood, and his mind has become freed from attachment to the passions. It is impossible that Yasa, the noble youth, should return to a worldly life to find enjoyment in lusts, as he did before, while he lived in his house. What if I were now to make the exercise of my miraculous power to cease. Then the Lord made the exercise of his miraculous power to cease. So the guild master, the householder, saw Yasa, the noble youth, seated, and on seeing him he said to Yasa, the noble youth, "Your mother, Yasa, my son, is filled with lamentation and grief; restore your mother to life." Then Yasa, the noble youth, looked at the Lord. And the Lord said to the guild master, the householder, "Now what do you think, householder? Yasa with imperfect knowledge and imperfect insight has perceived the Doctrine as you have, and on contemplating the stage of knowledge thus perceived and thus understood, his mind has become freed from attachment to the passions. Is it possible, householder, that Yasa should return to a worldly life to find enjoyment in lusts, as he did before, while he lived in his house?" "It is not possible, reverend sir." "Yasa, the noble youth, householder, with imperfect knowledge and imperfect insight has perceived the Doctrine as you have, and on contemplating the stage of knowledge thus perceived and thus understood, his mind has become freed from attachment to the passions. It is not possible, householder, that Yasa, the noble youth, should return to a worldly life to find enjoyment in lusts, as he did while he lived in his house." "It is gain, reverend sir, to Yasa, the noble youth, it is great gain to Yasa, the noble youth, reverend sir, that the mind of Yasa, the noble youth, should be freed from attachment to the passions. Let the reverend Lord consent to take food today from me with Yasa, the noble youth, as a junior brother." The Lord by his silence consented. And the guild master, perceiving the consent of the Lord, rose from his seat, saluted the Lord, passed round him, keeping his right side toward him, and departed. Then Yasa, the noble youth, soon after the guild master, the householder, was gone, said to the Lord, "Reverend sir, let me receive from the Lord the ordination of going forth (*pabbajā*), and of admission to the order (*upasampadā*)." "Come, bhikku," said the Lord, "the Doctrine is well taught, lead a holy life for the complete extinction of suffering." This was the ordination of this elder. At that time there were seven arahats in the world.

XI

ORDINATION BY THE THREEFOLD REFUGE

To this day the ordination of a Buddhist monk is an impressive ritual in whatever land performed. Its central declaration is that of taking refuge in the Buddha, his Doctrine (or Law), and his Order (i.e. the monastic community). In the following,[12] *Buddha is represented as authorizing his monks to confer ordination in different regions. It also indicates an early rapid spread of his Doctrine as he sent out disciples to teach it. (For a modern ordination in Siam see Appendix, page 177.)*

At that time the monks brought [to Buddha], from different regions and different countries, persons who desired to leave the world and be ordained, thinking: The Blessed One will confer on them the one and the other ordination. But the monks became tired [from the journey], and those also who desired to obtain the ordination. Now when the Blessed One was alone and had retired into solitude, the following consideration presented itself to his mind: The monks now bring to me from different regions and different countries persons who desire to obtain ordination, thinking: The Blessed One will confer on them the ordination. Now both the monks become tired, and those also who desire to obtain ordination. What if I were to grant permission to the monks, saying,

[12] From the Mahāvagga of the Vinaya Texts, in E. H. Brewster, *Life of Gotama the Buddha*, pp. 76-77.

Confer henceforth, monks, in the different regions and in different countries both modes of ordination yourselves.

And the Blessed One, having left his solitude in the evening, in consequence of that, and on this occasion, after having delivered a religious discourse, thus addressed the monks: "When I was alone, monks, and had retired into solitude, the following consideration presented itself to me: What if I were to permit . . . [as above].

"I grant you, monks, this permission: Confer henceforth in the different regions and in the different countries both modes of ordination yourselves [on those who desire to receive them]. And you ought, monks, to confer them in this way: Let him [who desires to receive ordination] first have his hair and beard cut off, let him put on yellow robes, adjust his upper robe so as to cover one shoulder, salute the feet of the monks [with his head], and sit down squatting; then let him raise his joined hands and tell him to say:

" 'I take my refuge in the Buddha, I take my refuge in the Dhamma, I take my refuge in the Sangha. And for the second time I take [as above . . . Sangha]. And for the third time I take my refuge in the Buddha, and for the third time I take my refuge in the Dhamma, and for the third time I take my refuge in the Sangha!'

"I prescribe, O monks, that the world be left and ordination given by the three times repeated declaration of taking refuge."

XII

CONVERSION OF THE TWO CHIEF DISCIPLES

Two disciples, formerly brāhmans, appear in Buddhist literature as eminent among the rest in ability and wisdom, and most possessed of intellectual sympathy with Buddha. Like the master himself they had left home to lead the religious life with one of the wandering teachers of the time, but without finding satisfaction. In the following,[13] they are converted on learning the Buddhist principle of the universal impermanence of existence—a thought which brings them to realization of "the sorrowless way."

At that time Sanjaya, a wandering ascetic (*paribbājaka*), resided at Rājagaha with a great retinue of wandering ascetics, with two hundred and fifty wandering ascetics. At that time Sāriputta and Moggallāna [two young brāhmans] led a religious life as followers of Sanjaya, the wandering ascetic; these had given their word to each other: He who first attains to the immortal shall tell the other one.

Now one day the venerable Assaji in the forenoon, having put on his under-robes, and having taken his alms-bowl and outer-robe, entered the city of Rājagaha for alms; his walking, turning back, regarding, looking, drawing [his arms] back, and stretching [them] out was decorous; he turned his eyes to the ground, and was dignified in deportment. Now the wandering ascetic Sāriputta saw the venerable Assaji, who went through Rājagaha for alms, whose walking, etc., was decorous, who kept his eyes to the ground, and was dignified in deportment. Seeing him, he thought: Indeed this person is one of those monks who are the worthy ones (arahats) in the world, or who have entered the path of arahatship. What if I were to approach this monk and to ask him, In whose name, friend, have you retired from the world? Who is your teacher? Whose dhamma do you profess?

Now the wandering ascetic Sāriputta thought, This is not the time to ask this monk; he has entered the inner yard of a house, walking for alms. What if I were to follow this monk step by step, according to the course recognized by those who want something?

And the venerable Assaji, having finished his alms-pilgrimage through Rājagaha, went back with the food he had received. Then the wandering ascetic Sāriputta went to the place where the venerable Assaji was; having approached him, he exchanged greetings with the venerable Assaji; having exchanged with him greetings

[13] From Mahāvagga I. Tr. by Brewster, *op. cit.*, pp. 94-96.

and complaisant words, he stationed himself at his side; standing at his side the wandering ascetic Sāriputta said to the venerable Assaji: "Your countenance, friend, is serene; your complexion is pure and bright. In whose name, friend, have you retired from the world? Who is your teacher? Whose dhamma do you profess?"

[Assaji replied]: "There is, friend, the great recluse, the Sakya's son, who has retired from the world, out of the Sakya clan; in this Blessed One's name have I retired from the world; this Blessed One is my teacher, and of the Dhamma of this Blessed One do I approve."

"And what, venerable Sir, is the doctrine which your teacher holds? And what does he preach to you?"

"I am only a young disciple, friend; I have but recently received ordination; and I have newly adopted this Dhamma and discipline. I cannot explain to you the Dhamma in detail; but I will tell you in short what it means."

Then Sāriputta, the wandering ascetic, said to the venerable Assaji: "So be it, friend, tell me as much or as little as you like, but tell me the meaning; I want just the meaning. Why make so much of the letter?"

Then the venerable Assaji pronounced to the wandering ascetic Sāriputta the following teaching of the Dhamma: Of all objects which proceed from a cause, the Tathāgata has explained the cause, and he has explained their cessation also; this is the doctrine of the great Samaṇa.

And Sāriputta, the wandering ascetic, after having heard this Dhamma text obtained the pure and spotless Dhamma-eye [namely]: Whatsoever is an arising thing, all that is a ceasing thing. [And he said]: "Even if this alone be the Dhamma, you have indeed seen the sorrowless way, lost sight of and passed over for many myriads of aeons."

Then the wandering ascetic Sāriputta went to the place where the wandering ascetic Moggallāna was. And the wandering ascetic Moggallāna saw the wandering ascetic Sāriputta coming from afar; seeing him, he said to the wandering ascetic Sāriputta: "Your countenance, friend, is serene; your complexion is pure and bright. Have you then really reached the immortal, friend?"

"Yes, friend, I have attained to the immortal."

"And how, friend, have you done so?"

. . . [Then Sāriputta told him of his meeting with Assaji.]

And the wandering ascetic Moggallāna, after having heard this Dhamma text, obtained the pure and spotless Dhamma-eye [that is the following knowledge]: Whatsoever is an arising thing, all that is a ceasing thing. [And Moggallāna said]: "Even if this alone be the Dhamma, indeed you have seen the sorrowless way, lost sight of and passed over for many myriads of aeons."

XIII

THE LAST DAYS AND DEATH OF BUDDHA

For forty-five years after his Great Enlightenment [14] Buddha carried on the work of teaching and organizing into a religious community his large and increasing number of followers. At times he journeyed among the cities and tribes where his doctrine spread, having always with him a group of his disciples. Among these was his relative and faithful attendant Ānanda. No chronological account of these labors exists. In a scripture known as the "Book of the Great Decease," however, events belonging to the last few months of the great teacher are described. Two passages are here selected.[15] One is the story of Buddha's acceptance of the hospitality of a humble lay disciple. The other recounts his last words and death.

I

BUDDHA'S VISIT TO CHUNDA

The Lord, after staying at Bhoganagara as long as he wished, said to the elder Ānanda, "Come, Ānanda, we will go to Pāvā."

[14] The year of the Great Enlightenment, according to E. J. Thomas, was 528 B.C.

[15] From Mahā-Parinibbāna-sutta. Tr. by E. J. Thomas, in his *Buddhist Scriptures,* pp. 109-117.

"Yes, reverend sir," the elder Ānanda replied. Then the Lord, with a great retinue of brethren, proceeded to Pāvā. There the Lord dwelt at Pāvā in the mango-grove of Chunda, who was of a family of smiths. Now Chunda the smith heard that the Lord had arrived at Pāvā and was dwelling in his mango-grove. So Chunda the smith approached the Lord, and, having approached, he saluted the Lord and sat down on one side. As he sat on one side the Lord instructed, aroused, incited, and gladdened him with a discourse on the Doctrine. Then Chunda the smith, instructed, aroused, incited, and gladdened by the discourse on the Doctrine, said to the Lord, "Let the reverend Lord accept food from me tomorrow with the retinue of brethren." By his silence the Lord assented. So Chunda the smith, perceiving the assent of the Lord, arose from his seat, saluted the Lord, and, passing around him to the right, went away.

The next day Chunda the smith caused to be prepared in his house excellent food, hard and soft, and much truffle, and caused it to be announced to the Lord: "It is time, reverend sir; the meal is ready." So the Lord, in the morning, dressed himself, took his bowl and robe, and with the retinue of brethren went to the abode of Chunda the smith. On arriving he sat on the appointed seat and said to Chunda the smith: "Serve me, Chunda, with the truffles that are prepared, and serve the retinue of brethren with the other hard and soft food prepared." "Yes, reverend sir," assented Chunda the smith, and served the Lord with the truffles prepared, and the retinue of brethren with the other hard and soft food. Then the Lord said to Chunda the smith: "The truffles that remain, Chunda, bury in a pit. I see no one in the world of gods and men, of Māra, of Brahma, or among ascetics and brāhmins, gods and men, by whom it could be eaten and properly digested, except by the Tathāgata." "Yes, reverend sir," assented Chunda, and, burying the remaining truffles in a pit, he approached the Lord, and, having approached, he saluted the Lord and sat down on one side. As he sat on one side, the Lord instructed, aroused, incited, and gladdened him with a discourse on the Doctrine, and then arose from his seat and departed.

Then there arose in the Lord, after he had eaten the food of

Chunda the smith, sharp pain and dysentery, and violent mortal pains set in. Conscious and self-possessed the Lord endured them without anxiety, and said to the elder Ānanda, "Come, Ānanda, let us go to Kusinārā." "Yes, reverend sir," the elder Ānanda assented.

II
THE DEATH OF BUDDHA

Then the Lord said to the elder Ānanda: "It may be, Ānanda, that you may think, 'Passed away is the utterance of the Master; we have a Master no more.' Not so, Ānanda, is it to be so regarded. The Doctrine and discipline which have been taught and laid down by me is the Master after my departure. And as now, Ānanda, the brethren address one another as 'friend,' after my departure they are not so to address them. An elder brother is to address a younger brother by his name, or family name, or the term 'friend,' and a younger brother is to address an elder brother as 'reverend sir' or 'elder.' Let the assembly, Ānanda, if it so wish, after my death, abolish some commands of minor importance. On Channa, Ānanda, after my departure the brahma-punishment is to be imposed." "What, reverend sir, is the brahma-punishment?" "The brother Channa, Ānanda, may say what he wishes, he is not to be addressed by the brethren, nor admonished, nor instructed."

Then the Lord addressed the brethren: "It may be that even a single brother may be in doubt or uncertainty about the Buddha, or the Doctrine, or the path, or the course of conduct. Ask, brethren; do not with regret say afterwards, 'The Master was face to face with us, and we could not ask the Lord face to face.'" At these words the brethren were silent. [A second time and a third time the Lord thus addressed the brethren.] And even a third time the brethren were silent. Then the Lord addressed the brethren: "It may be, brethren, that you do not ask out of reverence for the Master; let a friend tell it to his friend." At these words the brethren were silent. Then the elder Ānanda addressed the Lord: "Wonderful, reverend sir, marvelous, reverend sir, in this assembly of brethren there is not even a single brother who is in doubt or uncertainty about the Buddha, or the Doctrine, or the assembly, or the path, or the course of conduct." "With faith, Ānanda, have you spoken, and in this matter, Ānanda, the Tathāgata has the knowledge that in this assembly not even a single brother is in doubt or uncertainty about the Buddha, or the Doctrine, or the assembly, or the path, or the course of conduct. For in this assembly of five hundred brethren the lowest brother has entered the stream, is not liable to be born in a lower state of existence, is sure and destined to attain perfect knowledge." Then the Lord addressed the brethren: "Well then, brethren, I now exhort you. Impermanent are compound things; strive with earnestness." These were the last words of the Tathāgata.

Then the Lord reached the first Ecstasy, and ascending from the first he reached the second, from the second he reached the third, and from the third he reached the fourth. From the fourth he reached the abode of infinite space, from the Attainment of the abode of infinite space he reached the abode of infinite consciousness, from the Attainment of the abode of infinite consciousness he reached the abode of nothingness, from the Attainment of the abode of nothingness he reached the abode of neither perception nor non-perception, and from the Attainment of the abode of neither perception nor non-perception, he reached the destruction of sensation and perception. Then the elder Ānanda addressed the elder Anuruddha: "Reverend Anuruddha, the Lord has attained Nirvāṇa." "No, friend Ānanda, the Lord has not attained Nirvāṇa, he has attained the destruction of sensation and perception." Then the Lord from the Attainment of the destruction of sensation and perception reached the abode of neither perception nor non-perception; from the Attainment of the abode of neither perception nor non-perception he reached the abode of nothingness; from the Attainment of the abode of nothingness he reached the abode of infinite consciousness; from the Attainment of the abode of infinite consciousness he reached the abode of infinite space; from the Attainment of the abode of infinite space he reached the fourth Ecstasy; from the fourth the third, from the third the second, from the second the first, from the first the second, from the second the third, and from the third the fourth; and immediately after ascending from the fourth the Lord attained Nirvāṇa.

When the Lord attained Nirvāṇa, at the time of the Nirvāṇa, there was a great shaking of the earth, terrifying and frightful, and the drums of the gods resounded. When the Lord attained Nirvāṇa, at the time of the Nirvāṇa, Brahma Sahampati uttered this verse:

> All beings in the world must lose
> Their compound selves and disappear.
> So such a Master as was he,
> A man unrivaled in the world,
> The Lord endowed with all the powers,
> The All-wise, has Nirvāna reached.

When the Lord attained Nirvāṇa, at the time of the Nirvāṇa, Sakka, king of the gods, uttered this verse:

> Impermanent are compound things,
> Growth is their nature and decay;
> They grow up, and they cease again,
> Good is it when they pass away.

When the Lord attained Nirvāṇa, at the time of the Nirvāṇa, the elder Anuruddha uttered these verses:

> No longer breathed he in or out
> With firm-fixed mind, the Holy One,
> Free from desires, in peace resting,
> Then when the great Sage passed away.

> With mind unshaken, resolute,
> Did he endure the suffering.
> As the extinction of a flame,
> Even so was his mind's release.

When the Lord attained Nirvāṇa, at the time of the Nirvāṇa the elder Ānanda uttered this verse:

> Then was a terrifying dread,
> Then was a frightful awe and fear,
> When he adorned with all the signs,
> The All-wise One, Nirvāna reached.

PART TWO
PĀLI BUDDHIST LITERATURE: EARLY TEACHINGS

XIV

THE FIRE DISCOURSE

Transitoriness of all things connected with the world of sense and its desires is a recurrent theme in Buddha's teaching. Here it is set forth under the metaphor of fire,[1] possibly suggested by one of the jungle fires which still can be seen from a hillside near Gayā as they creep along the spurs of the Great Vindhyan mountain range.

The Lord having stayed at Uruvelā as long as he wished, went forward to Gayāsīsa with a great assembly of brethren, with a thousand brethren, who had all previously been ascetics. There the Lord addressed the brethren: "Everything, brethren, is on fire. How, brethren, is everything on fire? The eye, brethren, is on fire, visible objects are on fire, the faculty of the eye is on fire, the sense of the eye is on fire, and also the sensation, whether pleasant or unpleasant or both, which arises from the sense of sight, is on fire. With what is it on fire? With the fire of passion, of hate, of illusion is it on fire, with birth, old age, death, grief, lamentation, suffering, sorrow, and despair. Thus I declare. The ear is on fire, sounds are on fire [etc.]. . . . The nose is on fire, scents are on fire, the tongue is on fire, tastes are on fire, the body is on fire, objects of touch are on fire, the mind is on fire, mental objects are on fire, the faculty of the mind is on fire, the perception of the mind is on fire, the sensation, whether pleasant or unpleasant or both, which arises from the inner sense is on fire. With what is it on fire? With the fire of passion, of hate, of illusion is it on fire, with birth, old age, death, grief, lamentation, suffering, sorrow, and despair. Thus I declare.

[1] The passage is from the Mahāvagga, I, 21, in E. J. Thomas, *Buddhist Scriptures,* pp. 54-56. (Cf. J. G. Jennings, *The Vedāntic Buddhism of the Buddha,* 1948, p. xl.)

"The wise and noble disciple, brethren, perceiving this, is indifferent to the eyes, indifferent to visible objects, indifferent to the faculty of the eye, indifferent to sensation, whether pleasant or unpleasant or both, which arises from the sense of sight. He is indifferent to the ear, indifferent to sounds, indifferent to the nose, indifferent to scents, indifferent to the tongue, indifferent to tastes, indifferent to the body, indifferent to objects of touch, indifferent to the mind, indifferent to mental objects, indifferent to the faculty of the mind, indifferent to the perception of the mind, indifferent to the sensation, whether pleasant or unpleasant or both, which arises from the inner sense. And being indifferent he becomes free from passion, by absence of passion is he liberated, and when he is liberated the knowledge 'I am liberated' arises. Rebirth is destroyed, a religious life is lived, duty is done, and he knows there is nothing more for him in this state."

And when this exposition was spoken the minds of the thousand brethren were freed from the passions and liberated.

XV

ON BURSTING BONDS ASUNDER

An ideal of inner freedom and tranquillity, transcendence of the vicissitudes of existence, runs through all of Buddhist literature. Ignorant clinging to what is impermanent is seen as the source of suffering, giving rise to bonds or fetters which prevent the attainment of the higher life. How to break these bonds by following the path discovered by the Enlightened One is the theme of the following discourse.[2]

Thus have I heard: Once when the Lord was staying at Sāvatthī in Jeta's grove in Anāthapiṇḍika's pleasaunce, he addressed the

[2] Majjhima Nikāya, Sutta No. 64. Tr. by Lord Chalmers, in his *Further Dialogues of the Buddha,* Pt. I, pp. 308-311.

almsmen, saying: "Do you know the Five Bonds which chain men to the lower life here, as taught by me?"

"Yes, I do," said the reverend Mālunkyā-putta.

"And what is your knowledge of them?"

"One is views on personality; another is doubt; another is attachment to observances; fourth come lusts of the flesh; and the fifth is malevolence."

"To whom do you hear that I so taught the Five Bonds? Would not wanderers who profess other creeds confute you with the illustration from infancy? For a newborn babe, helpless on its back, is not conscious of personality at all, much less can it hold views on personality, its propensity to views on personality being latent only. Such an infant is not conscious of doctrines, much less can it have doubts about them, its propensity to doubt being latent only. Such an infant is not conscious of rules of conduct, much less can it be attached to observances, its propensity to such attachment being latent only. Such an infant is not conscious of lusts of the flesh, much less can passion arise within it, its sensual propensities being latent only. Such an infant is not conscious of fellow creatures, much less can it harbor malevolence toward them, its malevolent propensities being latent only. Would not wanderers who profess other creeds confute you, Mālunkyā-putta, with this illustration from infancy?"

At this point the reverend Ānanda exclaimed: "Now is the time for this, Lord; now is the time, Blessed One, for the Lord to impart teaching about the Five Bonds, to be treasured up from his lips by the almsmen."

"Give ear then, Ānanda, and listen," said the Lord; "and I will speak." Then to the listening Ānanda the Lord began:

"Take an uninstructed everyday man, who has no vision of the Noble and is unversed and untrained in their Noble Doctrine, who has no vision of the Excellent and is unversed and untrained in their Excellent Doctrine. Such a man's mind is beset and obsessed by delusions about personality; he knows no real escape therefrom; and these delusions about personality, if left to grow in strength, are a Bond to chain him to this lower life here. Just the same, too, happens with doubt, with attachment to rites, with sensuality, and with malevolence; all of which are likewise Bonds to chain him to this lower life here. On the other hand, the instructed disciple of the Noble—who has vision of the Noble and Excellent and is versed and trained in Noble and Excellent Doctrine—has a mind beset and obsessed by no delusions about personality and the rest of the Five Bonds; he knows the real escape therefrom; he discards each and all of them, with all propensities thereto.

"Without first treading the path and the course for getting rid of these Five Bonds, it is quite impossible for a man to know or discern or to get rid of them, any more than it is possible, without first cutting away bark and foliage, to cut the choice timber of a fine upstanding timber tree.

"But, if he has first trodden the path and the course for getting rid of these Five Bonds, it is possible for a man to know and discern and get rid of them, just as it is possible, after first cutting away bark and foliage, to cut the choice timber of the tree.

"Just as a weakling, coming to the Ganges in flood and thinking his arms can bear him across in safety to the further shore, would fail in the attempt—in just the same case is whosoever fails, when the doctrine of stilling personality is being preached, to embrace it, welcome it, cleave to it, and stand fast therein. This is the case of such men.

"But just as a strong man, coming to the Ganges in flood and thinking his arms can bear him across in safety to the further shore, would succeed in the attempt—in just the same case is whosoever succeeds, when the doctrine of stilling personality is being preached, in embracing it, welcoming it, cleaving to it, and standing fast therein. This is the case of such men.

"Now, what is the path and what is the course unto riddance of these Five Bonds which chain men to this lower world here? Take an almsman who, by aloofness from all ties, by eschewing wrong states of consciousness, and by quelling all lewdness of body, becomes divested of pleasures of sense and of wrong states of consciousness so that he develops and dwells in the First Ecstasy with all its zest and satisfaction—a state bred of inward aloofness but not divorced from observation and reflection. Whatsoever occurs as a visible shape, or feeling, or perception, or factors of being—all such mental phenomena he regards as transitory, as Ill, as disease, as pustulences, as pangs, as anguish, as maladies, as extraneous, as fleeting, as hollow, as non-self. He purges his mind of all such mental phenomena and applies it, so purged, to the state which is deathless, confident that what is really good and really excellent is the stilling of all factors of being, riddance from all ties, destruction of cravings, passionlessness, peace, Nirvāṇa. From this platform he attains to the extirpation of the cankers; or, if he does not attain to their definite extirpation, yet by his very passion for righteousness and by his very delight therein, he destroys the Five Bonds which chain him to this lower world here so that he will be translated hereafter to realms above, from which he will never return to earth.—Such is the path and such is the course unto riddance of these Five Bonds.

"Rising above observation and reflection, the almsman enters on, and abides in, the Second Ecstasy with all its zest and satisfaction—a state bred of rapt concentration, above all observation and reflection, a state whereby the heart is focused and tranquillity reigns within. And then follow the Third and Fourth ecstasies. Whatsoever occurs as a visible shape . . . riddance of these Five Bonds.

"Rising next altogether beyond perception of the visible, by ceasing to perceive sense reactions, and by not heeding perception of differences, the almsman reaches the idea of infinite space and so develops, and abides in, the plane of infinite space, and, in succession, the plane of infinite mind. Whatsoever occurs as a visible shape . . . riddance of these Five Bonds which chain men to the lower life here."

"If this, sir, be the path and the course unto riddance of these Five Bonds, how comes it that Deliverance is found by some through the heart and by others through the intellect?"

"I say it results from difference in their respective faculties."

Thus spoke the Lord. Glad at heart, the reverend Ānanda rejoiced in what the Lord had said.

XVI

THE QUESTIONS OF MĀLUNKYĀ-PUTTA

Metaphysical speculation was common among religious teachers in Buddha's day. He himself, although aware of the many theories abroad, discouraged preoccupation with such questions and would not discuss them with his disciples. His reason was that they do not conduce to solution of the great problem of human life, deliverance from desire and sorrow. A classic statement of his attitude is the following.[3]

Thus have I heard: The Lord was once dwelling near Sāvatthī, at Jetavana in the park of Anāthapiṇḍika. Now the elder Mālunkyā-putta had retired from the world, and as he meditated the thought arose: These theories have been left unexplained by the Lord, set aside, and rejected, whether the world is eternal or not eternal, whether the world is finite or not, whether the soul (life) is the same as the body, or whether the soul is one thing and the body another, whether a Buddha (*Tathāgata*) exists after death or does not exist after death, whether a Buddha both exists and does not exist after death, and whether a Buddha is nonexistent and not nonexistent after death—these things the Lord does not explain to me, and that he does not explain them to me does not please me, it does not suit me. I will approach the Lord and ask about this matter. . . . If the Lord does not explain to me, I will give up the training and return to a worldly life.

[When Mālunkyā-putta had approached and put his questions, the Lord replied:] "Now did I, Mālunkyā-putta, ever say to you, Come, Mālunkyā-putta, lead a religious life with me, and I will explain to you whether the world is eternal or not eternal [and so on with the other questions]?" "You did not, reverend sir." "Anyone, Mālunkyā-putta, who should say, I will not lead a religious life with the Lord, until the Lord explains to me whether

[3] Majjhima Nikāya, Sutta 63. Tr. by E. J. Thomas, in his *Buddhist Scriptures*, pp. 64-67.

the world is eternal or not eternal [etc.] . . . that person would die, Mālunkyā-putta, without its being explained. It is as if a man had been wounded by an arrow thickly smeared with poison, and his friends, companions, relatives, and kinsmen were to get a surgeon to heal him, and he were to say, I will not have this arrow pulled out until I know by what man I was wounded, whether he is of the warrior caste, or a brāhmin, or of the agricultural, or the lowest caste. Or if he were to say, I will not have this arrow pulled out until I know of what name or family the man is . . . or whether he is tall, or short, or of middle height . . . or whether he is black, or dark, or yellowish . . . or whether he comes from such and such a village, or town, or city . . . or until I know whether the bow with which I was wounded was a chāpa or a kodanda, or until I know whether the bow-string was of swallow-wort, or bamboo fiber, or sinew, or hemp, or of milk-sap tree, or until I know whether the shaft was from a wild or cultivated plant . . . or whether it was feathered from a vulture's wing or a heron's or a hawk's, or a peacock's, or a sithilahanu-bird's . . . or whether it was wrapped round with the sinew of an ox, or of a buffalo, or of a ruru-deer, or of a monkey . . . or until I know whether it was an ordinary arrow, or a razor-arrow, or a vekanda. or an iron arrow, or a calf-tooth arrow, or one of a karavīra leaf. That man would die, Mālunkyā-putta, without knowing all this.

"It is not on the view that the world is eternal, Mālunkyā-putta, that a religious life depends; it is not on the view that the world is not eternal that a religious life depends. Whether the view is held that the world is eternal, or that the world is not eternal, there is still rebirth, there is old age, there is death, and grief, lamentation, suffering, sorrow, and despair, the destruction of which even in this life I announce. It is not on the view that the world is finite. . . . It is not on the view that a Tathāgata exists after death. . . . Therefore, Mālunkyā-putta, consider as unexplained what I have not explained, and consider as explained what I have explained. And what, Mālunkyā-putta, have I not explained? Whether the world is eternal I have not explained, whether the world is not eternal . . . whether a Tathāgata is both nonexistent and not nonexistent after death I have not explained

And why, Mālunkyā-putta, have I not explained this? Because this, Mālunkyā-putta, is not useful, it is not concerned with the principle of a religious life, does not conduce to aversion, absence of passion, cessation, tranquillity, supernatural faculty, perfect knowledge, Nirvāṇa, and therefore I have not explained it.

"And what, Mālunkyā-putta, have I explained? Suffering have I explained, the cause of suffering, the destruction of suffering, and the path that leads to the destruction of suffering have I explained. For this, Mālunkyā-putta, is useful, this is concerned with the principle of a religious life; this conduces to aversion, absence of passion, cessation, tranquillity, supernatural faculty, perfect knowledge, Nirvāṇa, and therefore have I explained it. Therefore, Mālunkyā-putta, consider as unexplained what I have not explained, and consider as explained what I have explained." Thus spoke the Lord, and with joy the elder Mālunkyā-putta applauded the words of the Lord.

XVII

THE QUESTIONS OF VACCHAGOTTA

As in the preceding selection, Buddha is here shown declining to answer questions of a metaphysical character.[4] *The point of special interest is the refusal to state definitely what becomes of the saint after death. This silence of the master gave room for diverse views on the subject to flourish among Buddha's followers later.*

"Vaccha, the view that the world is eternal is a jungle, a wilderness, a theatrical show, a perversion, a fetter, and is coupled with suffering, destruction, despair, and pain, and does not tend to aversion, absence of passion, cessation, tranquillity, supernatural faculty, perfect knowledge, Nirvāṇa. . . . Considering it disadvan-

[4] From the Majjhima-Nikāya, Sutta 72. Tr. by E. J. Thomas, *op. cit.,* pp. 71-74.

tageous, Vaccha, I have accordingly adopted none of these views."

"But has Gotama any view?"

"The Tathāgata, Vaccha, is free from views, for this is what the Tathāgata holds: form, the cause of form, the destruction of form, sensation, the cause of sensation, the destruction of sensation, perception, the aggregates of qualities, consciousness, how they arise and perish. Therefore with the destruction of, and indifference toward, and the ceasing and abandonment of all imaginings, all agitations, all false views of the self or of anything belonging to a self, the Tathāgata is liberated, thus I say."

"But where is the monk reborn, sir Gotama, whose mind is thus liberated?"

"It does not fit the case, Vaccha, to say he is reborn."

"Then, sir Gotama, he is not reborn."

"It does not fit the case, Vaccha, to say he is not reborn."

"Then, sir Gotama, he is both reborn and not reborn."

"It does not fit the case, Vaccha, to say he is both reborn and not reborn."

"Then, sir Gotama, he is neither reborn nor not reborn."

"It does not fit the case, Vaccha, to say he is neither reborn nor not reborn." . . .

"In this matter, sir Gotama, I feel in a state of ignorance and confusion, and the small amount of faith that I had in Gotama through a former conversation has now disappeared."

"Enough of your ignorance and confusion, Vaccha, for deep is this Doctrine, difficult to be seen and comprehended, good, excellent, beyond the sphere of reasoning, subtle, intelligible only to the wise. It is difficult to be understood by you, who hold other views, another faith, other inclinations, another discipline, and have another teacher. Therefore, Vaccha, I will ask you this, and do you explain it as you may please. Do you think, Vaccha, that if a fire were burning before you, you would know that a fire was burning before you?"

"If a fire were burning before me, sir Gotama, I should know that a fire was burning before me."

"And if someone asked you on what the fire burning before you depends, how would you explain it?" . . .

"I should say that this fire which is burning before me depends on its clinging to grass and sticks."

"If the fire before you were to go out, would you know that the fire before you had gone out?"

"If the fire before me were to go out, I should know that the fire had gone out."

"And if someone were to ask you, Vaccha, in what direction has the fire gone which has gone out, to the east, west, north, or south, if you were thus asked, how would you explain it?"

"It does not fit the case, sir Gotama, to say so, for the fire burned through depending on its clinging to grass and sticks, and through its consuming this, and not getting any other, it is without food, and comes to be what is called extinct."

"And just so, Vaccha, that form by which one would assert the existence of a Tathāgata has ceased, it is uprooted, it is pulled up like a taliput-palm, made nonexistent, and not liable to arise again in the future. The Tathāgata, who is released from what is called 'form,' is deep, immeasurable, hard to fathom, and like a great ocean. It does not fit the case to say he is born again, to say he is not born again, to say he is both born again and not born again, or to say he is neither born again nor not born again. . . ."

At these words the wandering ascetic Vaccha said to the Lord, "Sir Gotama, it is as if there were a great sal-tree near a village or town, and from the nature of its growth its branches and leaves were to fall, the pieces of bark, and fibrous wood; and afterwards, with the disappearance of these branches, leaves, pieces of bark, and small fiber, it were to be established, pure in its strength. Even so does this discourse of Gotama, with the disappearance of branches, leaves, pieces of bark and small fiber, stand established, pure in its strength. Wonderful, sir Gotama, wonderful, sir Gotama, it is as if one were setting up what was overturned, or revealing what was hidden, or showing the way to one who was lost, or putting a lamp in the dark—they who have eyes see visible things— even so has the Doctrine been expounded by Gotama in many ways. I go to Gotama as a refuge, and to the Doctrine, and to the assembly of brethren. May Gotama take me as a lay disciple from this day forth while my life lasts, who have come to him for refuge."

XVIII

CONSCIOUSNESS A PROCESS ONLY

In the following passage [5] Buddha is represented as firmly opposing the idea of a permanent identical self, transmigrating from one existence to another. By contrast it is maintained that consciousness is not some kind of permanent entity, but a changing process arising from causal conditions. The first view issues in self-concern and selfish deeds: the second leads to selflessness and deliverance from sorrow. Though the point is not here developed, it is to be observed that the conception of consciousness as a causal process allows more stress on moral responsibility as implied in the Eightfold Path of right living.

Thus have I heard: Once when the Lord was staying at Sāvatthī in Jeta's grove in Anāthapiṇḍika's pleasaunce, an almsman named Sāti, a fisherman's son, came to entertain the pernicious view that, as he understood the Lord's teaching of the Doctrine, our consciousness runs on and continues without break of identity.

Hearing of this, a number of almsmen went to ask Sāti whether he was correctly reported as entertaining a view so pernicious. Certainly he did, was his avowal. Then those almsmen plied Sāti with question, inquiry, and argument so as to wean him from his error. Do not, they said, do not say this; do not misrepresent the Lord; there are no grounds whatever for such a charge; the Lord would not say such a thing. [On the contrary], in many a figure has it been laid down by the Lord that consciousness only arises by causation and that without assignable conditions consciousness does not come about. But say what they would, Sāti would not yield to their expostulations, but stoutly held and clung to his pernicious view that, as he understood the Lord's teaching of the Doctrine, our consciousness ran on and continued without break of identity.

[5] From Majjhima Nikāya, Sutta 38. Tr. by Lord Chalmers, in his *Further Dialogues of the Buddha,* Pt. I, pp. 183-189.

So when they had failed to wean Sāti from his error, the almsmen went to the Lord and laid the whole of the facts before him; and he sent an almsman to summon Sāti to his presence.

When Sāti had duly come and had taken his seat to one side after due obeisance, the Lord asked him whether he was correctly reported as entertaining this pernicious view. Yes, Sāti certainly did hold it. Said the Lord: "What, Sāti, is the nature of this consciousness?"

"Sir, it is that speaking and sentient [Self] which experiences the ripened fruits of good and bad conduct in this or that earlier existence."

"Pray, to whom, foolish man, do you aver that I ever so taught the doctrine? Have I not, foolish man, laid it down in many a figure that consciousness only arises by causation and that without assignable conditions consciousness does not come about? And yet you, foolish man, employ what you have misunderstood not only to misrepresent me, but also to undermine yourself and breed for yourself a store of demerit—to your lasting hurt and harm."

Turning then to the almsmen, the Lord said: "What think you? Has this Sāti, the fisherman's son, got even a spark of illumination in this doctrine and rule?"

"How could he, sir? For it is not the fact."

Hereat, Sāti sat silent and glum, with his shoulders hunched up and eyes downcast, much exercised in his mind but finding no words to utter. Seeing him in this plight, the Lord said to him: "And now, foolish man, you shall be shown up in respect of this pernicious view of yours; I will question the almsmen."

Accordingly, the Lord said to them: "Do you understand me ever to have preached the Doctrine in the sense of this almsman Sāti, who employs what he has misunderstood not only to misrepresent me, but also to undermine himself and to breed for himself a store of demerit, to his lasting hurt and harm?"

"No, sir. For in many a figure has the Lord taught us that consciousness only arises by causation and that without assignable conditions consciousness does not come about."

"Quite right; you rightly understand my teaching; for, indeed,

I have, as you say, so taught in many a figure. Yet here is this Sāti, the fisherman's son, who employs . . . hurt and harm.

"Whatsoever form of consciousness arises from an assignable condition is known by that condition's name. If the eye and visible shapes condition consciousness, that is called visual consciousness; and so on with the senses and objects of hearing, smelling, tasting, and touch, and of mind with its mental objects. It is just like a fire, where that which makes the fire burn gives the fire its name. Wood makes a wood-fire, sticks a stick-fire, grass a grass-fire, cowdung a cowdung-fire, husks a husk-fire, and rubbish a rubbish-fire. In just the same way, every form of consciousness arising from an assignable cause is known by that condition's name. Do you recognize, almsmen, an organism as such?"

"Yes, sir."

"Do you recognize it as the product of a particular sustenance?"

"Yes, sir."

"Do you recognize that, by the cessation of its particular sustenance, the organism's nature makes for cessation?"

"Yes, sir."

"Does doubt of the fact of each of these three points lead to perplexity thereon?"

"Yes, sir."

"Does recognition of the fact as it really is, in the fullness of knowledge, dispel that perplexity in each case?"

"Yes, sir."

"In each of the three cases, is there right recognition, if it be in the fullness of knowledge of the fact as it really is?"

"Yes, sir."

"If you insist on hugging and cherishing this pure and undefiled conception and if you refuse to relinquish or part with it, could you realize a state of consciousness to cross with, but not to keep, as in the allegory of the raft?"

"No, sir."

"Could you realize that allegory if, while hugging and cherishing your conception, you were yet ready to relinquish and part with it?"

"Yes, sir."

"There are four sustenances which either maintain existing organisms or help those yet to be: First of these is material sustenance, coarse or delicate; contact is the second; cogitation is the third; and perception is the fourth. The derivation, origin, birth, and production of all four sustenances alike is craving. Craving in its turn arises from feeling, feeling from contact, contact from the sensory domains, sensory domains from name-and-form, name-and-form from consciousness, consciousness from plastic forces, and these latter from ignorance. Thus, ignorance conditions plastic forces, which condition consciousness, which conditions name-and-form, which condition the sensory domains, which condition contact, which conditions feeling, which conditions craving, which conditions dependence, which conditions becoming, which conditions birth, which conditions decay and death, with the distractions of grief, tribulation, and pain of body and mind. This is the uprising of all that makes up the sum of Ill.

"I have said that birth conditions decay and death. Does it, or does it not, condition them? Or how stands the matter?"

"Birth, sir, does condition decay and death; and that is how the matter stands."

"I have said that becoming conditions birth. Does it, or does it not? Or how stands the matter?"

"Becoming, sir, does condition birth; and that is how the matter stands."

[Similar paragraphs for dependence, etc., down to ignorance.]

"Good, almsmen; very good. You and I then agree in affirming that: *This* being so, *that* comes about; if *this* arises, so does *that;* thus, ignorance conditions plastic force . . . [etc., as above] . . . the sum of Ill.

"So too it is by the entire and passionless cessation of ignorance that the plastic forces cease . . . [etc., for the successive links in the chain, down to] . . . the distractions of grief, tribulation, and pain of body and mind. This is the cessation of all that makes up the sum of Ill.

"I have said that by the cessation of birth, decay and death cease. Do they, or do they not? Or how stands the matter?"

"By the cessation of birth, decay and death also cease, sir; and that is how the matter stands."

[Similar paragraphs for becoming, etc., down to ignorance.] "Good; very good. You and I then agree in affirming that: *This* not being so, *that* comes not about; if *this* ceases, so does *that;* thus with the cessation of ignorance the plastic forces cease . . . [etc., for the successive links in the chain, down to] . . . cessation of all that makes up the sum of Ill.

"Now, almsmen, would you, knowing and seeing all this, hark back to the past, wondering whether you were, or whether you were not, in existence during bygone ages; what you were in those ages; how you fared then; and from what you passed on to what else?"

"No, sir."

"Or, would you, knowing and seeing all this, hark forward to the future, wondering whether you will, or whether you will not, be in existence during the ages to come; what you will be in those ages; how you will fare then; and from what you will pass on to what else?"

"No, sir."

"Or, again, would you, knowing and seeing all this, be perplexed in the present about whether or not you exist, what and how you are, whence your being came, and whither it will go?"

"No, sir."

"Would you, knowing and seeing all this, say, We revere our teacher, and it is because of our reverence for him that we affirm this?"

"No, sir."

"Would you, knowing and seeing all this, say, Oh, we were told this by a recluse or recluses; we do not affirm it ourselves?"

"No, sir."

"Would you, knowing and seeing all this, look out for another teacher?"

"No, sir."

"Would you, knowing and seeing all this, frequent the ritual and shows and functions of the ordinary run of recluses and brāhmins as being of the essence?"

"No, sir."

"Do you not affirm only what you have of yourselves known, seen, and discerned?"

"Yes, sir."

"Quite right, almsmen. You have by me been introduced to this Doctrine, which is immediate in its gifts here and now, which is open to all, which is a guide onward, which can be mastered for himself by every intelligent man. All I have said was to bring out that this Doctrine was immediate in its gifts here and now, open to all, a guide onward to be mastered for himself by every intelligent man."

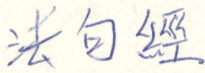

XIX

THE DHAMMAPADA [6]

Buddhist wisdom in its most readily understood form appears in the famous scripture bearing the above title. The meaning of the title has been variously understood by scholars, but most conveniently and simply it can be translated as "Scripture Verses." For here, drawn from many parts of the Pāli canon, are moral sayings which were regarded by early Buddhists as utterances of the founder of their religion. The selection and arrangement of these under suitable topics puts in strong relief the cherished ideals for the conduct of life. Who was responsible for this we do not know. It is certain, however, that among classics of the world's ethical literature The Dhammapada is entitled to high rank.

CHAPTER I: THE TWIN VERSES

All that we are is the result of what we have thought: it is founded on our thoughts, it is made up of our thoughts. If a man speaks or acts with an evil thought, pain follows him, as the wheel follows the foot of the ox that draws the carriage.

[6] Tr. by F. Max Müller, in *The Sacred Books of the East*, Vol. X, Pt. 1. Müller's extensive notes and the numbering of the verses are here omitted.

All that we are is the result of what we have thought: it is founded on our thoughts, it is made up of our thoughts. If a man speaks or acts with a pure thought, happiness follows him, like a shadow that never leaves him.

"He abused me, he beat me, he defeated me, he robbed me"—in those who harbor such thoughts hatred will never cease.

"He abused me, he beat me, he defeated me, he robbed me"—in those who do not harbor such thoughts hatred will cease.

For hatred does not cease by hatred at any time; hatred ceases by love—this is an old rule.

The world does not know that we must all come to an end here; but those who know it, their quarrels cease at once.

He who lives looking for pleasures only, his senses uncontrolled, immoderate in his food, idle, and weak, Māra (the tempter) will certainly overthrow him, as the wind throws down a weak tree.

He who lives without looking for pleasures, his senses well-controlled, moderate in his food, faithful, and strong, him Māra will certainly not overthrow, any more than the wind throws down a rocky mountain.

He who wishes to put on the yellow dress without having cleansed himself from sin, who disregards also temperance and truth, is unworthy of the yellow dress.

But he who has cleansed himself from sin, is well grounded in all virtues, and endowed also with temperance and truth: he is indeed worthy of the yellow dress.

They who imagine truth in untruth, and see untruth in truth, never arrive at truth, but follow vain desires.

They who know truth in truth, and untruth in untruth, arrive at truth and follow true desires.

As rain breaks through an ill-thatched house, passion will break through an unreflecting mind.

As rain does not break through a well-thatched house, passion will not break through a well-reflecting mind.

The evildoer mourns in this world, and he mourns in the next; he mourns in both. He mourns and suffers when he sees the evil result of his own work.

The virtuous man delights in this world, and he delights in the next; he delights in both. He delights and rejoices, when he sees the purity of his own work.

The evildoer suffers in this world, and he suffers in the next; he suffers in both. He suffers when he thinks of the evil he has done; he suffers more when going on the evil path.

The virtuous man is happy in this world, and he is happy in the next; he is happy in both. He is happy when he thinks of the good he has done; he is still more happy when going on the good path.

The thoughtless man, even if he can recite a large portion of the law, but is not a doer of it, has no share in the priesthood, but is like a cowherd counting the cows of others.

The follower of the law, even if he can recite only a small portion of the law, but, having forsaken passion and hatred and foolishness, possesses true knowledge and serenity of mind, he, caring for nothing in this world or that to come, has indeed a share in the priesthood.

CHAPTER II: ON EARNESTNESS

Earnestness is the path of immortality (Nirvāṇa); thoughtlessness the path of death. Those who are in earnest do not die; those who are thoughtless are as if dead already.

Having understood this clearly, those who are advanced in earnestness delight in earnestness, and rejoice in the knowledge of the elect.

These wise people, meditative, steady, always possessed of strong powers, attain to Nirvāṇa, the highest happiness.

If an earnest person has roused himself, if he is not forgetful, if his deeds are pure, if he acts with consideration, if he restrains himself, and lives according to law—then his glory will increase.

By rousing himself, by earnestness, by restraint and control, the wise man may make for himself an island which no flood can overwhelm.

Fools follow after vanity. The wise man keeps earnestness as his best jewel.

Follow not after vanity, nor after the enjoyment of love and lust! He who is earnest and meditative obtains ample joy.

When the learned man drives away vanity by earnestness, he, the wise, climbing the terraced heights of wisdom, looks down upon the fools: free from sorrow he looks upon the sorrowing crowd, as one that stands on a mountain looks down upon them that stand upon the plain.

Earnest among the thoughtless, awake among the sleepers, the wise man advances like a racer, leaving behind the hack.

By earnestness did Maghavan (Indra) rise to the lordship of the gods. People praise earnestness; thoughtlessness is always blamed.

A bhikshu (mendicant) who delights in earnestness, who looks with fear on thoughtlessness, moves about like fire, burning all his fetters, small or large.

A bhikshu who delights in reflection, who looks with fear on thoughtlessness, cannot fall away from his perfect state—he is close upon Nirvāṇa.

CHAPTER III: THOUGHT

As a fletcher makes straight his arrow, a wise man makes straight his trembling and unsteady thought, which is difficult to guard, difficult to hold back.

As a fish taken from his watery home and thrown on the dry ground, our thought trembles all over in order to escape the dominion of Māra, the tempter.

It is good to tame the mind, which is difficult to hold in and flighty, rushing wherever it lists; a tamed mind brings happiness.

Let the wise man guard his thoughts, for they are difficult to perceive, very artful, and they rush wherever they list: thoughts well guarded bring happiness.

Those who bridle their mind, which travels far, moves about alone, is without a body, and hides in the chamber of the heart, will be free from the bonds of Māra, the tempter.

If a man's faith is unsteady, if he does not know the true law, if his peace of mind is troubled, his knowledge will never be perfect.

If a man's thoughts are not dissipated, if his mind is not perplexed, if he has ceased to think of good or evil, then there is no fear for him while he is watchful.

Knowing that this body is fragile like a jar, and making his thought firm like a fortress, one should attack Māra, the tempter, with the weapon of knowledge, one should watch him when conquered, and should never rest.

Before long, alas! this body will lie on the earth, despised, without understanding, like a useless log.

Whatever a hater may do to a hater, or an enemy to an enemy, a wrongly-directed mind will do him greater mischief.

Not a mother, not a father, will do so much, nor any other relatives; a well-directed mind will do us greater service.

CHAPTER IV: FLOWERS

Who shall overcome this earth, and the world of Yama, the lord of the departed, and the world of the gods? Who shall find out the plainly shown path of virtue, as a clever man finds the right flower?

The disciple will overcome the earth, and the world of Yama, and the world of the gods. The disciple will find out the plainly shown path of virtue, as a clever man finds the right flower.

He who knows that this body is like froth, and has learned that it is as unsubstantial as a mirage, will break the flower-pointed arrow of Māra, and never see the king of death.

Death carries off a man who is gathering flowers, and whose mind is distracted, as a flood carries off a sleeping village.

Death subdues a man who is gathering flowers, and whose mind is distracted, before he is satiated in his pleasures.

As the bee collects nectar and departs without injuring the flower, or its color or scent, so let a sage dwell in his village.

Not the perversities of others, not their sins of commission or omission, but his own misdeeds and negligences should a sage take notice of.

Like a beautiful flower, full of color, but without scent, are the fine but fruitless words of him who does not act accordingly.

But, like a beautiful flower, full of color and full of scent, are the fine and fruitful words of him who acts accordingly.

As many kinds of wreaths can be made from a heap of flowers, so many good things may be achieved by a mortal when once he is born.

The scent of flowers does not travel against the wind, nor that of sandal wood, or of Tagara and Mallikā flowers; but the odor of good people travels even against the wind; a good man pervades every place.

Sandal wood or Tagara, a lotus flower, or a Vassikī, among these sorts of perfumes, the perfume of virtue is unsurpassed.

Mean is the scent that comes from Tagara and sandal wood; the perfume of those who possess virtue rises up to the gods as the highest.

Of the people who possess these virtues, who live without thoughtlessness, and who are emancipated through true knowledge, Māra, the tempter, never finds the way.

As on a heap of rubbish cast upon the highway the lily will grow full of sweet perfume and delight, thus among those who are mere rubbish the disciple of the truly enlightened Buddha shines forth by his knowledge above the blinded worldling.

CHAPTER V: THE FOOL

Long is the night to him who is awake; long is a mile to him who is tired; long is life to the foolish who do not know the true law.

If a traveler does not meet with one who is his better, or his equal, let him firmly keep to his solitary journey; there is no companionship with a fool.

"These sons belong to me, and this wealth belongs to me"—with such thoughts a fool is tormented. He himself does not belong to himself; how much less sons and wealth?

The fool who knows his foolishness is wise at least so far. But a fool who thinks himself wise, he is called a fool indeed.

If a fool be associated with a wise man even all his life. he will perceive the truth as little as a spoon perceives the taste of soup.

If an intelligent man be associated for one minute only with a wise man, he will soon perceive the truth, as the tongue perceives the taste of soup.

Fools of poor understanding have themselves for their greatest enemies, for they do evil deeds which bear bitter fruits.

That deed is not well done of which a man must repent, and the reward of which he receives crying and with a tearful face.

No, that deed is well done of which a man does not repent, and the reward of which he receives gladly and cheerfully.

As long as the evil deed done does not bear fruit, the fool thinks it is like honey; but when it ripens, then the fool suffers grief.

Let a fool month after month eat his food [like an ascetic] with the tip of a blade of Kusa-grass, yet is he not worth the sixteenth particle of those who have well weighed the law.

An evil deed, like newly-drawn milk, does not turn suddenly; smouldering, like fire covered by ashes, it follows the fool.

And when the evil deed, after it has become known, turns to sorrow for the fool, then it destroys his bright lot, nay, it cleaves his head.

Let the fool wish for a false reputation, for precedence among the bhikshus, for lordship in the convents, for worship among other people!

"May both the layman and he who has left the world think that this is done by me; may they be subject to me in everything which is to be done or is not to be done"—thus is the mind of the fool, and his desire and pride increase.

"One is the road that leads to wealth, another the road that leads to Nirvāṇa"—if the bhikshu, the disciple of Buddha, has learned this, he will not yearn for honor, he will strive after separation from the world.

CHAPTER VI: THE WISE MAN

If you see a man who shows you what is to be avoided, who administers reproofs, and is intelligent, follow that wise man as you would one who tells of hidden treasures; it will be better, not worse, for him who follows him.

Let him admonish, let him teach, let him forbid what is improper!—he will be beloved of the good; by the bad he will be hated.

Do not have evildoers for friends, do not have low people for friends: have virtuous people for friends, have for friends the best of men.

He who drinks in the law lives happily with a serene mind: the sage rejoices always in the law, as preached by the elect.

Well-makers lead the water wherever they like; fletchers bend the arrow; carpenters bend a log of wood; wise people fashion themselves.

As a solid rock is not shaken by the wind, wise people falter not amidst blame and praise.

Wise people, after they have listened to the laws, become serene, like a deep, smooth, and still lake.

Good men indeed walk warily under all circumstances; good men speak not out of a desire for sensual gratification; whether touched by happiness or sorrow wise people never appear elated or depressed.

If, whether for his own sake, or for the sake of others, a man wishes neither for a son, nor for wealth, nor for lordship, and if he does not wish for his own success by unfair means, then he is good, wise, and virtuous.

Few are there among men who arrive at the other shore (become arhats); the other people here run up and down the shore.

But those who, when the law has been well preached to them, follow the law, will pass over the dominion of death, however difficult to cross.

A wise man should leave the dark state of ordinary life, and follow the bright state of the bhikshu. After going from his home to a homeless state, he should in his retirement look for enjoyment where enjoyment seemed difficult. Leaving all pleasures behind, and calling nothing his own, the wise man should purge himself of all the troubles of the mind.

Those whose mind is well grounded in the seven elements of knowledge, who without clinging to anything rejoice in freedom from attachment, whose appetites have been conquered, and who are full of light, they are free even in this world.

CHAPTER VII: THE VENERABLE

There is no suffering for him who has finished his journey and abandoned grief, who has freed himself on all sides and thrown off all fetters.

They exert themselves with their thoughts well collected, they do not tarry in their abode; like swans who have left their lake, they leave their house and home.

Men who have no riches, who live on recognized food, who have perceived void and unconditioned freedom (Nirvāṇa), their path is difficult to understand, like that of birds in the air.

He whose appetites are stilled, who is not absorbed in enjoyment, who has perceived void and unconditioned freedom (Nirvāṇa), his path is difficult to understand, like that of birds in the air.

The gods even envy him whose senses, like horses well broken in by the driver, have been subdued, who is free from pride, and free from appetites; such a one who does his duty is tolerant like the earth, or like a threshold; he is like a lake without mud; no new births are in store for him.

His thought is quiet, quiet are his word and deed, when he has obtained freedom by true knowledge, when he has thus become a quiet man.

The man who is free from credulity, but knows the uncreated, who has cut all ties, removed all temptations, renounced all desires, he is the greatest of men.

In a hamlet or in a forest, on sea or on dry land, wherever venerable persons (arahanta) dwell, that place is delightful.

Forests are delightful; where the world finds no delight, there the passionless will find delight, for they look not for pleasures.

CHAPTER VIII: THE THOUSANDS

Even though a speech be a thousand (words), but made up of senseless words, one word of sense is better, which if a man hears, he becomes quiet.

Even though a gāthā (poem) be a thousand (words), but made up of senseless words, one word of a gāthā is better, which if a man hears, he becomes quiet.

Though a man recite a hundred gāthās made up of senseless words, one word of the law is better, which if a man hears, he becomes quiet.

If one man conquer in battle a thousand times a thousand men, and if another conquer himself, he is the greatest of conquerors.

One's own self conquered is better than all other people; not even a god, a Gandharva, not Māra (with Brāhman), could change into defeat the victory of a man who has vanquished himself, and always lives under restraint.

If a man for a hundred years sacrifice month by month with a thousand, and if he but for one moment pay homage to a man whose soul is grounded in true knowledge, better is that homage than a sacrifice for a hundred years.

If a man for a hundred years worship Agni (fire) in the forest, and if he but for one moment pay homage to a man whose soul is grounded in true knowledge, better is that homage than sacrifice for a hundred years.

Whatever a man sacrifice in this world as an offering or as an oblation for a whole year in order to gain merit, the whole of it is not worth a quarter of a farthing; reverence shown to the righteous is better.

He who always greets and constantly reveres the aged, four things will increase to him: life, beauty, happiness, power.

But he who lives a hundred years, vicious and unrestrained—a life of one day is better if a man is virtuous and reflecting.

And he who lives a hundred years, ignorant and unrestrained—a life of one day is better if a man is wise and reflecting.

And he who lives a hundred years, idle and weak—a life of one day is better if a man has attained firm strength.

And he who lives a hundred years, not seeing beginning and end—a life of one day is better if a man sees beginning and end.

And he who lives a hundred years, not seeing the immortal place—a life of one day is better if a man sees the immortal place.

And he who lives a hundred years, not seeing the highest law—a life of one day is better if a man sees the highest law.

CHAPTER IX: EVIL

A man should hasten toward the good, and should keep his thought away from evil; if a man does what is good slothfully, his mind delights in evil.

If a man commits a sin, let him not do it again; let him not delight in sin—the accumulation of evil is painful.

If a man does what is good, let him do it again; let him delight in it—the accumulation of good is delightful.

Even an evildoer sees happiness so long as his evil deed does not ripen; but when his evil deed ripens, then does the evildoer see evil.

Even a good man sees evil days so long as his good deed does not ripen; but when his good deed ripens, then does the good man see good things.

Let no man think lightly of evil, saying in his heart, It will not come nigh unto me. Even by the falling of water drops a water pot is filled; the fool becomes full of evil, even if he gather it little by little.

Let no man think lightly of good, saying in his heart, It will not come nigh unto me. Even by the falling of water drops a water pot is filled; the wise man becomes full of good, even if he gather it little by little.

Let a man avoid evil deeds, as a merchant, if he has few companions and carries much wealth, avoids a dangerous road; as a man who loves life avoids poison.

He who has no wound on his hand may touch poison with his hand; poison does not affect one who has no wound; nor is there evil for one who does not commit evil.

If a man offend a harmless, pure, and innocent person, the evil falls back upon that fool, like light dust thrown up against the wind.

Some people are born again; evildoers go to hell; righteous people go to heaven; those who are free from all worldly desires attain Nirvāṇa.

Not in the sky, not in the midst of the sea, not if we enter into the clefts of the mountains, is there known a spot in the whole world where a man might be freed from an evil deed.

Not in the sky, not in the midst of the sea, not if we enter into the clefts of the mountains, is there known a spot in the whole world where death could not overcome the mortal.

CHAPTER X: PUNISHMENT

All men tremble at punishment, all men fear death; remember that you are like unto them, and do not kill, nor cause slaughter.

All men tremble at punishment, all men love life; remember that you are like unto them, and do not kill, nor cause slaughter.

He who, seeking his own happiness, punishes or kills beings who also long for happiness, will not find happiness after death.

He who, seeking his own happiness, does not punish or kill beings who also long for happiness, will find happiness after death.

Do not speak harshly to anyone; those who are spoken to will answer you in the same way. Angry speech is painful: blows for blows will touch you.

If, like a shattered metal plate (gong), you utter nothing, then you have reached Nirvāṇa; anger is not known to you.

As a cowherd with his staff drives his cows into the stable, so do age and death drive the life of men.

A fool does not know when he commits his evil deeds; but the wicked man burns by his own deeds, as if burned by fire.

He who inflicts pain on innocent and harmless persons will soon come to one of these ten states:

He will have cruel suffering, loss, injury of the body, heavy affliction, or loss of mind.

A misfortune coming from the king, or a fearful accusation, or loss of relations, or destruction of treasures.

Lightning-fire will burn his houses; and when his body is destroyed, the fool will go to hell.

Not nakedness, not plaited hair, not dirt, not fasting, or lying on the earth; not rubbing with dust, not sitting motionless, can purify a mortal who has not overcome desires.

He who, though dressed in fine apparel, exercises tranquillity, is quiet, subdued, restrained, chaste, and has ceased to find fault with all other beings, he indeed is a brāhmana, an ascetic (*sramana*), a friar (*bhikshu*).

Is there in this world any man so restrained by shame that he does not provoke reproof, as a noble horse the whip?

Like a noble horse when touched by the whip, be ye strenuous and eager, and by faith, by virtue, by energy, by meditation, by discernment of the law, you will overcome this great pain, perfect in knowledge and in behavior, and never forgetful.

Well-makers lead the water wherever they like; fletchers bend the arrow; carpenters bend a log of wood; good people fashion themselves.

CHAPTER XI: OLD AGE

How is there laughter, how is there joy, as this world is always burning? Do you not seek a light, ye who are surrounded by darkness?

Look at this dressed-up lump, covered with wounds, joined together, sickly, full of many schemes, but which has no strength, no hold!

This body is wasted, full of sickness, and frail; this heap of corruption breaks to pieces, life indeed ends in death.

After one has looked at those gray bones, thrown away like gourds in the autumn, what pleasure is there left in life!

After a stronghold has been made of the bones, it is covered with flesh and blood, and there dwell in it old age and death, pride and deceit.

The brilliant chariots of kings are destroyed, the body also approaches destruction, but the virtue of good people never approaches destruction—thus do the good say to the good.

A man who has learned little, grows old like an ox; his flesh grows, but his knowledge does not grow.

Looking for the maker of this tabernacle, I have run through a course of many births, not finding him; and painful is birth again and again. But now, maker of the tabernacle, you have been seen; you shall not make up this tabernacle again. All your rafters are broken, your ridge pole is sundered; the mind, approaching the Eternal (*Visankhāra, Nirvāṇa*), has attained to the extinction of all desires.

Men who have not observed proper discipline, and have not gained wealth in their youth, perish like old herons in a lake without fish.

Men who have not observed proper discipline, and have not gained wealth in their youth, lie, like broken bows, sighing after the past.

CHAPTER XII: SELF

If a man hold himself dear, let him watch himself carefully; during one at least out of the three watches a wise man should be watchful.

Let each man direct himself first to what is proper, then let him teach others; thus a wise man will not suffer.

If a man make himself as he teaches others to be, then, being himself well subdued, he may subdue others; for one's own self is difficult to subdue.

Self is the lord of self, who else could be the lord? With self well subdued, a man finds a lord such as few can find.

The evil done by one's self, self-forgotten, self-bred, crushes the foolish, as a diamond breaks even a precious stone.

He whose wickedness is very great brings himself down to that state where his enemy wishes him to be, as a creeper does with the tree which it surrounds.

Bad deeds, and deeds hurtful to ourselves, are easy to do; what is beneficial and good, that is very difficult to do.

The foolish man who scorns the rule of the venerable (arhat), of the elect (ariya), of the virtuous, and follows a false doctrine, he bears fruit to his own destruction, like the fruits of the Katthaka reed.

By one's self the evil is done, by one's self one suffers; by one's self evil is left undone; by one's self one is purified. The pure and the impure stand and fall by themselves, no one can purify another.

Let no one forget his own duty for the sake of another's, however great; let a man, after he has discerned his own duty, be always attentive to his duty.

CHAPTER XIII: THE WORLD

Do not follow the evil law! Do not live on in thoughtlessness! Do not follow false doctrine! Be not a friend of the world.

Rouse yourself! Do not be idle! Follow the law of virtue! The virtuous rest in bliss in this world and in the next.

Follow the law of virtue; do not follow that of sin. The virtuous rest in bliss in this world and in the next.

Look upon the world as you would on a bubble, look upon it as you would on a mirage: the king of death does not see him who thus looks down upon the world.

Come, look at this world, glittering like a royal chariot; the foolish are immersed in it, but the wise do not touch it.

He who formerly was reckless and afterward became sober, brightens up this world, like the moon when freed from clouds.

He whose evil deeds are covered by good deeds, brightens up this world, like the moon when freed from clouds.

This world is dark, few only can see here; a few only go to heaven, like birds escaped from the net.

The swans go on the path of the sun, they go miraculously through the ether; the wise are led out of this world when they have conquered Māra and his train.

If a man has transgressed the one law, and speaks lies, and scoffs at another world, there is no evil he will not do.

The uncharitable do not go to the world of the gods; fools only do not praise liberality; a wise man rejoices in liberality, and through it becomes blessed in the other world.

Better than sovereignty over the earth, better than going to heaven, better than lordship over all worlds, is the reward of Sotāpatti, the first step in holiness.

CHAPTER XIV: THE BUDDHA—THE AWAKENED

He whose conquest cannot be conquered again, into whose conquest no one in this world enters, by what track can you lead him, the Awakened, the Omniscient, the trackless?

He whom no desire with its snares and poisons can lead astray, by what track can you lead him, the Awakened, the Omniscient, the trackless?

Even the gods envy those who are awakened and not forgetful, who are given to meditation, who are wise, and who delight in the repose of retirement from the world.

Difficult to obtain is the conception of men, difficult is the life of mortals, difficult is the hearing of the True Law, difficult is the birth of the Awakened [the attainment of Buddhahood].

Not to commit any sin, to do good, and to purify one's mind, that is the teaching of all the Awakened.

The Awakened call patience the highest penance, long-suffering the highest Nirvāṇa; for he is not an anchorite (*pravragita*) who strikes others, he is not an ascetic (*śramaṇa*) who insults others.

Not to blame, not to strike, to live restrained under the law, to be moderate in eating, to sleep and sit alone, and to dwell on the highest thoughts—this is the teaching of the Awakened.

There is no satisfying lusts, even by a shower of gold pieces; he who knows that lusts have a short taste and cause pain, he is wise; even in heavenly pleasures he finds no satisfaction; the disciple who is fully awakened delights only in the destruction of all desires.

Men, driven by fear, go to many a refuge, to mountains and forests, to groves and sacred trees.

But that is not a safe refuge, that is not the best refuge; a man is not delivered from all pains after having gone to that refuge.

He who takes refuge with Buddha, the Law, and the Church; he who, with clear understanding, sees the Four Holy Truths·

pain, the origin of pain, the destruction of pain, and the Eightfold Holy Way that leads to the quieting of pain—that is the safe refuge, that is the best refuge; having gone to that refuge, a man is delivered from all pain.

A supernatural person (a Buddha) is not easily found: he is not born everywhere. Wherever such a sage is born, that race prospers.

Happy is the arising of the Awakened, happy is the teaching of the True Law, happy is peace in the Church, happy is the devotion of those who are at peace.

He who pays homage to those who deserve homage, whether the Awakened (Buddhas) or their disciples, those who have overcome the host of evils, and crossed the flood of sorrow—he who pays homage to such as have found deliverance and know no fear, his merit can never be measured by anyone.

CHAPTER XV: HAPPINESS

We live happily indeed, not hating those who hate us! among men who hate us we dwell free from hatred! We live happily indeed, free from ailments among the ailing! among men who are ailing let us dwell free from ailments!

We live happily indeed, free from greed among the greedy! among men who are greedy let us dwell free from greed!

We live happily indeed, though we call nothing our own! We shall be like the bright gods, feeding on happiness!

Victory breeds hatred, for the conquered is unhappy. He who has given up both victory and defeat, he, the contented, is happy.

There is no fire like passion; there is no losing throw like hatred; there is no pain like this body; there is no happiness higher than rest.

Hunger is the worst of diseases, the elements of the body the greatest evil; if one knows this truly, that is Nirvāṇa, the highest happiness.

Health is the greatest of gifts, contentedness the best riches; trust is the best of relationships, Nirvāṇa the highest happiness.

He who has tasted the sweetness of solitude and tranquillity is free from fear and free from sin, while he tastes the sweetness of drinking in the law.

The sight of the elect (ariya) is good, to live with them is always happiness; if a man does not see fools, he will be truly happy.

He who walks in the company of fools suffers a long way; company with fools, as with an enemy, is always painful; company with the wise is pleasure, like meeting with kinsfolk.

Therefore, one ought to follow the wise, the intelligent, the learned, the much enduring, the dutiful, the elect; one ought to follow such a good and wise man, as the moon follows the path of the stars.

CHAPTER XVI: PLEASURE

He who gives himself to vanity, and does not give himself to meditation, forgetting the real aim of life and grasping at pleasure, will in time envy him who has exerted himself in meditation.

Let no man ever cling to what is pleasant, or to what is unpleasant. Not to see what is pleasant is pain, and it is pain to see what is unpleasant.

Let, therefore, no man love anything; loss of the beloved is evil. Those who love nothing, and hate nothing, have no fetters.

From pleasure comes grief, from pleasure comes fear; he who is free from pleasure knows neither grief nor fear.

From affection comes grief, from affection comes fear; he who is free from affection knows neither grief nor fear.

From lust comes grief, from lust comes fear; he who is free from lust knows neither grief nor fear.

From love comes grief, from love comes fear; he who is free from love knows neither grief nor fear.

From greed comes grief, from greed comes fear; he who is free from greed knows neither grief nor fear.

He who possesses virtue and intelligence, who is just, speaks the truth, and does what is his own business, him the world will hold dear.

He in whom a desire for the Ineffable (Nirvāṇa) has sprung up, who in his mind is satisfied, and whose thoughts are not bewildered by love, he is called ūrdhvamsrotas (carried upwards by the stream).

Kinsmen, friends, and lovers salute a man who has been long away and returns safe from afar.

In like manner his good works receive him who has done good and has gone from this world to the other—as kinsmen receive a friend on his return.

CHAPTER XVII: ANGER

Let a man leave anger, let him forsake pride, let him overcome all bondage! No sufferings befall the man who is not attached to name-and-form, and who calls nothing his own.

He who holds back rising anger like a rolling chariot, him I call a real driver; other people are but holding the reins.

Let a man overcome anger by love, let him overcome evil by good; let him overcome the greedy by liberality, the liar by truth!

Speak the truth; do not yield to anger; give, if you are asked for little: by these three steps you will go near the gods.

The sages who injure nobody, and who always control their body, they will go to the unchangeable place (Nirvāṇa), where, if they have gone, they will suffer no more.

Those who are ever watchful, who study day and night, and who strive after Nirvāṇa, their passions will come to an end.

This is an old saying, O Atula, this is not as if of today: "They blame him who sits silent, they blame him who speaks much, they also blame him who says little; there is no one on earth who is not blamed."

There never was, there never will be, nor is there now, a man who is always blamed, or a man who is always praised.

But he whom those who discriminate praise continually day after day, as without blemish, wise, rich in knowledge and virtue, who would dare to blame him, like a coin made of gold from the Gambū river? Even the gods praise him, he is praised even by Brāhman.

Beware of bodily anger, and control your body! Leave the sins of the body, and with your body practice virtue!

Beware of the anger of the tongue, and control your tongue! Leave the sins of the tongue, and practice virtue with your tongue!

Beware of the anger of the mind, and control your mind! Leave the sins of the mind, and practice virtue with your mind!

The wise who control their body, who control their tongue, the wise who control their mind, are indeed well controlled.

CHAPTER XVIII: IMPURITY

You are now like a sear leaf, the messengers of death (Yama) have come near to you; you stand at the door of your departure, and you have no provision for your journey.

Make yourself an island, work hard, be wise! When your impurities are blown away, and you are free from guilt, you will enter into the heavenly world of the elect (ariya).

Your life has come to an end, you are come near to death (Yama), there is no resting place for you on the road, and you have no provision for your journey.

Let a wise man blow off the impurities of himself, as a smith blows off the impurities of silver, one by one, little by little, and from time to time.

As the impurity which springs from the iron, when it springs from it, destroys it, thus do a transgressor's own works lead him to the evil path.

The taint of prayers is nonrepetition; the taint of houses, nonrepair; the taint of complexion is sloth; the taint of a watchman, thoughtlessness.

Bad conduct is the taint of woman, niggardliness the taint of a benefactor; tainted are all evil ways, in this world and in the next.

But there is a taint worse than all taints—ignorance is the greatest taint. O mendicants! throw off that taint and become taintless!

Life is easy to live for a man who is without shame: a crow hero, a mischief-maker, an insulting, bold, and wretched fellow.

But life is hard to live for a modest man, who always looks for what is pure, who is disinterested, quiet, spotless, and intelligent.

He who destroys life, who speaks untruth, who in the world takes what is not given him, who goes to another man's wife; and the man who gives himself to drinking intoxicating liquors, he, even in this world, digs up his own root.

O man, know this, that the unrestrained are in a bad state; take care that greediness and vice do not bring you to grief for a long time!

The world gives according to their faith or according to their pleasure: if a man frets about the food and the drink given to others, he will find no rest either by day or by night.

He in whom that feeling is destroyed, and taken out with the very root, finds rest by day and by night.

There is no fire like passion, there is no shark like hatred, there is no snare like folly, there is no torrent like greed.

The fault of others is easily perceived, but that of one's self is difficult to perceive; a man winnows his neighbor's faults like chaff, but his own fault he hides, as a cheat hides the bad die from the player.

If a man looks after the faults of others and is always inclined to be offended, his own passions will grow, and he is far from the destruction of passions.

There is no path through the air; a man is not a samaṇa outwardly. The world delights in vanity; the Tathāgatas (the Buddhas) are free from vanity.

There is no path through the air; a man is not a samaṇa outwardly. No creatures are eternal; but the Awakened (Buddhas) are never shaken.

CHAPTER XIX: THE JUST

A man is not just if he carries a matter by violence; no, he who distinguishes both right and wrong, who is learned and guides others, not by violence, but by the same law, being a guardian of the law and intelligent, he is called just.

A man is not learned because he talks much; he who is patient, free from hatred and fear, he is called learned.

A man is not a supporter of the law because he talks much; even if a man has learned little, but sees the law bodily, he is a supporter of the law, a man who never neglects the law.

A man is not an elder because his head is gray; his age may be ripe, but he is called old-in-vain.

He in whom there is truth, virtue, pity, restraint, moderation, he who is free from impurity and is wise, he is called an Elder.

An envious, stingy, dishonest man does not become respectable by means of much talking only, or by the beauty of his complexion.

He in whom all this is destroyed, and taken out with the very root, he, when freed from hatred, is called respectable.

Not by tonsure does an undisciplined man who speaks falsehood become a samaṇa; can a man be a samaṇa who is still held captive by desire and greediness?

He who always quiets the evil, whether small or large, he is called a samaṇa (a quiet man), because he has quieted all evil.

A man is not a mendicant (bhikshu) simply because he asks others for alms; he who adopts the whole law is a bhikshu, not he who only begs.

He who is above good and evil, who is chaste, who with care passes through the world, he indeed is called a bhikshu.

A man is not a muni because he observes silence if he is foolish and ignorant; but the wise who, as with the balance, chooses the good and avoids evil, he is a muni, and is a muni thereby; he who in this world weighs both sides is called a muni.

A man is not an elect (ariya) because he injures living creatures; because he has pity on all living creatures, therefore is a man called ariya.

Not only by discipline and vows, not only by much learning, not by entering into a trance, not by sleeping alone, do I earn the happiness of release which no worldling can know. O bhikshu, he who has obtained the extinction of desires has obtained confidence.

CHAPTER XX: THE WAY

The best of ways is the Eightfold; the best of truths the Four Words; the best of virtues passionlessness; the best of men he who has eyes to see.

This is the way, there is no other that leads to the purifying of intelligence. Go on this path! This is the confusion of Māra, the tempter.

If you go on this way, you will make an end of pain—the way preached by me, when I had understood the removal of the thorns in the flesh.

You yourself must make an effort. The Tathāgatas (Buddhas) are only preachers. The thoughtful who enter the way are freed from the bondage of Māra.

All created things perish—he who knows and sees this becomes passive in pain; this is the way to purity.

All created things are grief and pain—he who knows and sees this becomes passive in pain; this is the way that leads to purity.

All forms are unreal—he who knows and sees this becomes passive in pain; this is the way that leads to purity.

He who does not rouse himself when it is time to rise, who, though young and strong, is full of sloth, whose will and thought are weak, that lazy and idle man never finds the way to knowledge.

Watching his speech, well restrained in mind, let a man never commit any wrong with his body! Let a man but keep these three roads of action clear, and he will achieve the way which is taught by the wise.

Through zeal knowledge is gained, through lack of zeal knowledge is lost; let a man who knows this double path of gain and loss thus place himself that knowledge may grow.

Cut down the whole forest of desires, not a tree only! Danger comes out of the forest of desires. When you have cut down both the forest of desires and its undergrowth, then, bhikshus, you will be rid of the forest and of desires!

So long as the desire of man toward women, even the smallest, is not destroyed, so long is his mind in bondage, as the calf that drinks milk is to its mother.

Cut out the love of self, like an autumn lotus, with your hand! Cherish the road of peace. Nirvāṇa has been shown by Sugata (Buddha).

"Here I shall dwell in the rain, here in winter and summer—" thus the fool meditates, and does not think of death.

Death comes and carries off that man, honored for his children and flocks, his mind distracted, as a flood carries off a sleeping village.

Sons are no help, nor a father, nor relations; there is no help from kinsfolk for one whom death has seized.

A wise and well-behaved man who knows the meaning of this should quickly clear the way that leads to Nirvāṇa.

CHAPTER XXI: MISCELLANEOUS

If by leaving a small pleasure one sees a great pleasure, let a wise man leave small pleasure and look to the great.

He who, by causing pain to others, wishes to obtain pleasure for himself, he, entangled in the bonds of hatred, will never be free from hatred.

What ought to be done is neglected, what ought not to be done is done; the desires of unruly, thoughtless people are always increasing.

But they whose whole watchfulness is always directed to their body, who do not follow what ought not to be done, and who steadfastly do what ought to be done, the desires of such watchful and wise people will come to an end.

A true brāhmana goes scatheless, though he have killed father and mother, and two valiant kings, though he has destroyed a kingdom with all its subjects.

A true brāhmana goes scatheless, though he have killed father and mother, and two holy kings, and an eminent man besides.

The disciples of Gotama (Buddha) are always well awake, and their thoughts day and night are always set on Buddha.

The disciples of Gotama are always well awake, and their thoughts day and night are always set on the Law.

The disciples of Gotama are always well awake, and their thoughts day and night are always set on the Church.

The disciples of Gotama are always well awake, and their thoughts day and night are always set on their body.

The disciples of Gotama are always well awake, and their mind day and night always delights in compassion.

The disciples of Gotama are always well awake, and their mind day and night always delights in meditation.

It is hard to leave the world to become a friar, it is hard to enjoy the world; hard is the monastery, painful are the houses; painful it is to dwell with equals to share everything in common, and the itinerant mendicant is beset with pain. Therefore let no man be an itinerant mendicant, and he will not be beset with pain.

A man full of faith, if endowed with virtue and glory, is respected, whatever place he may choose.

Good people shine from afar, like the snowy mountains; bad people are not seen, like arrows shot by night.

Sitting alone, lying down alone, walking alone without ceasing, and alone subduing himself, let a man be happy near the edge of a forest.

CHAPTER XXII: THE DOWNWARD COURSE

He who says what is not goes to hell; he also who, having done a thing, says I have not done it. After death both are equal: they are men with evil deeds in the next world.

Many men whose shoulders are covered with the yellow gown are ill-conditioned and unrestrained; such evildoers by their evil deeds go to hell.

Better it would be to swallow a heated iron ball, like flaring fire, than that a bad unrestrained fellow should live on the charity of the land.

Four things does a reckless man gain who covets his neighbor's wife—demerit; an uncomfortable bed; thirdly, punishment; and lastly, hell.

There is demerit, and the evil way to hell; there is the short pleasure of the frightened in the arms of the frightened, and the king imposes heavy punishment; therefore let no man think of his neighbor's wife.

As a grass-blade, if badly grasped, cuts the arm, badly practiced asceticism leads to hell.

An act carelessly performed, a broken vow, and hesitating obedience to discipline, all this brings no great reward.

If anything is to be done, let a man do it, let him attack it vigorously! A careless pilgrim only scatters the dust of his passions more widely.

An evil deed is better left undone, for a man repents of it afterwards; a good deed is better done, for having done it one does not repent.

Like a well-guarded frontier fort, with defenses within and without, so let a man guard himself. Not a moment should escape, for they who allow the right moment to pass suffer pain when they are in hell.

They who are ashamed of what they ought not to be ashamed of, and are not ashamed of what they ought to be ashamed of, such men, embracing false doctrines, enter the evil path.

They who fear when they ought not to fear, and fear not when they ought to fear, such men, embracing false doctrines, enter the evil path.

They who see sin where there is no sin, and see no sin where there is sin, such men, embracing false doctrines, enter the evil path.

They who see sin where there is sin, and no sin where there is no sin, such men, embracing the true doctrine, enter the good path.

CHAPTER XXIII: THE ELEPHANT

Silently I endured abuse as the elephant in battle endures the arrow sent from the bow; for the world is ill-natured.

They lead a tamed elephant to battle, the king mounts a tamed elephant; the tamed is the best among men, he who silently endures abuse.

Mules are good, if tamed, and noble Sindhu horses, and elephants with large tusks; but he who tames himself is better still.

For with these animals does no man reach the untrodden country (Nirvāṇa), where a tamed man goes on a tamed animal—on his own well-tamed self.

The elephant called Dhanapālaka, his temples running with pungent sap, and who is difficult to hold, does not eat a morsel when bound; the elephant longs for the elephant grove.

If a man becomes fat and a great eater, if he is sleepy and rolls himself about, that fool, like a hog fed on grains, is born again and again.

This mind of mine went formerly wandering about as it liked, as it listed, as it pleased; but I shall now hold it in thoroughly, as the rider who holds the hook holds in the furious elephant.

Be not thoughtless, watch your thoughts! Draw yourself out of the evil way, like an elephant sunk in mud.

If a man find a prudent companion who walks with him, is wise, and lives soberly, he may walk with him, overcoming all dangers, happy, but considerate.

If a man find no prudent companion who walks with him, is wise, and lives soberly, let him walk alone, like a king who has left his conquered country behind—like an elephant in the forest.

It is better to live alone: there is no companionship with a fool; let a man walk alone, let him commit no sin, with few wishes, like an elephant in the forest.

If the occasion arises, friends are pleasant; enjoyment is pleasant, whatever be the cause; a good work is pleasant in the hour of death; the giving up of all grief is pleasant.

Pleasant in the world is the state of a mother, pleasant the state of a father, pleasant the state of a samaṇa, pleasant the state of a brāhmana.

Pleasant is virtue lasting to old age, pleasant is a faith firmly rooted; pleasant is attainment of intelligence, pleasant is avoiding of sins.

CHAPTER XXIV: THIRST

The thirst of a thoughtless man grows like a creeper; he runs from life to life, like a monkey seeking fruit in the forest.

Whomsoever this fierce poisonous thirst overcomes, in this world, his sufferings increase like the abounding Bīrana grass.

But from him who overcomes this fierce thirst, difficult to be conquered in this world, sufferings fall off, like waterdrops from a lotus leaf.

This salutary word I tell you: "Do ye, as many as are here assembled, dig up the root of thirst, as he who wants the sweet-scented Usīra root must dig up the Bīrana grass, that Māra, the tempter, may not crush you again and again, as the stream crushes the reeds."

As a tree, even though it has been cut down, is firm so long as its root is safe, and grows again, thus, unless the feeders of thirst are destroyed, this pain of life will return again and again.

He whose thirty-six streams are strongly flowing in the channels of pleasure, the waves—his desires which are set on passion—will carry away that misguided man.

The channels run everywhere, the creeper of passion stands sprouting; if you see the creeper springing up, cut its root by means of knowledge.

A creature's pleasures are extravagant and luxurious; given up to pleasure and deriving happiness, men undergo again and again birth and decay.

Beset with lust, men run about like a snared hare; held in fetters and bonds, they undergo pain for a long time, again and again.

Beset with lust, men run about like a snared hare; let therefore the mendicant drive out thirst by striving after passionlessness for himself.

He who, having got rid of the forest of lust (after having reached Nirvāṇa), gives himself over to forest-life (to lust), and who, when free from the forest (from lust), runs to the forest (to lust), look at that man—though free, he runs into bondage!

Wise people do not call that a strong fetter which is made of iron, wood, or hemp; passionately strong is the care for precious stones and rings, for sons and a wife.

That fetter wise people call strong which drags down, yields, but is difficult to undo; after having cut this at last, people leave the world, free from cares, and leaving the pleasures of love behind.

Those who are slaves to passions, run down the stream of desires, as a spider runs down the web which he has made himself; when they have cut this, at last, wise people go onward, free from cares, leaving all pain behind.

Give up what is before, give up what is behind, give up what is between, when you go to the other shore of existence; if your mind is altogether free, you will not again enter into birth and decay.

If a man is tossed about by doubts, full of strong passions, and yearning only for what is delightful, his thirst will grow more and more, and he will indeed make his fetters strong.

If a man delights in quieting doubts, and, always reflecting, dwells on what is not delightful, he certainly will remove, nay, he will cut the fetter of Māra.

He who has reached the consummation, who does not tremble, who is without thirst and without sin, he has broken all the thorns of life—this will be his last body.

He who is without thirst and without affection, who understands the words and their interpretation, who knows the order of letters (those which are before and which are after), he has received his last body, he is called the great sage, the great man.

"I have conquered all, I know all, in all conditions of life I am free from taint; I have left all, and through the destruction of thirst I am free; having learned myself, whom should I indicate as my teacher?"

The gift of the Law exceeds all gifts; the sweetness of the Law exceeds all sweetness; the delight in the Law exceeds all delights; the extinction of thirst overcomes all pain.

Riches destroy the foolish, if they look not for the other shore; the foolish by his thirst for riches destroys himself, as if he were destroying others.

The fields are damaged by weeds, mankind is damaged by passion: therefore a gift bestowed on the passionless brings great reward.

The fields are damaged by weeds, mankind is damaged by hatred: therefore a gift bestowed on those who do not hate brings great reward.

The fields are damaged by weeds, mankind is damaged by vanity: therefore a gift bestowed on those who are free from vanity brings great reward.

The fields are damaged by weeds, mankind is damaged by lust: therefore a gift bestowed on those who are free from lust brings great reward.

CHAPTER XXV: THE BHIKSHU

Restraint in the eye is good, good is restraint in the ear; in the nose restraint is good, good is restraint in the tongue.

In the body restraint is good, good is restraint in speech; in thought restraint is good, good is restraint in all things. A bhikshu, restrained in all things, is freed from all pain.

He who controls his hand, he who controls his feet, he who controls his speech, he who is well controlled, he who delights inwardly, who is collected, who is solitary and content, him they call bhikshu.

The bhikshu who controls his mouth, who speaks wisely and calmly, who teaches the meaning and the Law, his word is sweet.

He who dwells in the Law, delights in the Law, meditates on the Law, recollects the Law: that bhikshu will never fall away from the true Law.

Let him not despise what he has received, nor ever envy others: a mendicant who envies others does not obtain peace of mind.

A bhikshu who, though he receives little, does not despise what he has received, even the gods will praise him if his life is pure and if he is not slothful.

He who never identifies himself with name-and-form, and does not grieve over what is no more, he indeed is called a bhikshu.

The bhikshu who behaves with kindness, who is happy in the Doctrine of Buddha, will reach the quiet place (Nirvāṇa), happiness arising from the cessation of natural inclinations.

O bhikshu, empty this boat! if emptied, it will go quickly; having cut off passion and hatred, you will go to Nirvāṇa.

Cut off the five fetters, leave the five, rise above the five. A bhikshu who has escaped from the five fetters, he is called Oghatinna (saved from the flood.)

Meditate, O bhikshu, and be not heedless! Do not direct your thought to what gives pleasure, that you may not for your heedlessness have to swallow the iron ball in hell, and that you may not cry out when burning—"This is pain."

Without knowledge there is no meditation, without meditation there is no knowledge: he who has knowledge and meditation is near unto Nirvāṇa.

A bhikshu who has entered his empty house, and whose mind is tranquil, feels a more than human delight when he sees the Law clearly.

As soon as he has considered the origin and destruction of the elements of the body, he finds happiness and joy which belong to those who know the immortal (Nirvāṇa).

And this is the beginning here for a wise bhikshu: watchfulness over the senses, contentedness, restraint under the Law; keep noble friends whose life is pure, and who are not slothful.

Let him live in charity, let him be perfect in his duties; then in the fullness of delight he will make an end of suffering.

As the Vassikā plant shed its withered flowers, men should shed passion and hatred, O ye bhikshus!

The bhikshu whose body and tongue and mind are quieted, who is collected, and has rejected the baits of the world, he is called quiet.

Rouse yourself by yourself, examine yourself by yourself, thus self-protected and attentive will you live happily, O bhikshu!

For self is the lord of self, self is the refuge of self; therefore curb yourself as the merchant curbs a noble horse.

The bhikshu, full of delight, who is happy in the Doctrine of Buddha will reach the quiet place (Nirvāṇa), happiness consisting in the cessation of natural inclinations.

He who, even as a young bhikshu, applies himself to the Doctrine of Buddha, brightens up this world, like the moon when free from clouds.

CHAPTER XXVI: THE BRĀHMANA

Stop the stream valiantly, drive away the desires, O brāhmana! When you have understood the destruction of all that was made, you will understand that which was not made.

If the brāhmana has reached the other shore in both laws, in restraint and contemplation, all bonds vanish from him who has obtained knowledge.

He for whom there is neither the hither nor the further shore, nor both—him, the fearless and unshackled, I call indeed a brāhmana.

He who is thoughtful, blameless, settled, dutiful, without passions, and who has attained the highest end, him I call indeed a brāhmana.

The sun is bright by day, the moon shines by night, the warrior is bright in his armor, the brāhmana is bright in his meditation; but Buddha, the Awakened, is bright with splendor day and night.

Because a man is rid of evil, therefore he is called brāhmana; because he walks quietly, therefore he is called samaṇa; because he has sent away his own impurities, therefore he is called pravragita (*pabbagita,* a pilgrim).

No one should attack a brāhmana, but no brāhmana, if attacked, should let himself fly at his aggressor! Woe to him who strikes a brāhmana, more woe to him who flies at his aggressor!

It advantages a brāhmana not a little if he holds his mind back from the pleasures of life; the more all wish to injure has vanished, the more all pain will cease.

Him I call indeed a brāhmana who does not offend by body, word, or thought, and is controlled on these three points.

He from whom he may learn the Law, as taught by the Well-Awakened (Buddha), him let him worship assiduously, as the brāhmana worships the sacrificial fire.

A man does not become a brāhmana by his plaited hair, by his family, or by birth; in whom there is truth and righteousness, he is blessed, he is a brāhmana.

What is the use of plaited hair, O fool! what of the raiment of goatskins? Within you there is ravening, but the outside you make clean.

The man who wears dirty raiments, who is emaciated and covered with veins, who meditates alone in the forest, him I call indeed a brāhmana.

I do not call a man a brāhmana because of his origin or of his mother. He is indeed arrogant, and he is wealthy: but the poor who is free from all attachments, him I call indeed a brāhmana.

Him I call indeed a brāhmana who, after cutting all fetters, never trembles, is free from bonds and unshackled.

Him I call indeed a brāhmana who, after cutting the strap and the thong, the rope with all that pertains to it, has destroyed all obstacles and is awakened.

Him I call indeed a brāhmana who, though he has committed no offense, endures reproach, stripes, and bonds; who has endurance for his force and strength for his army.

Him I call indeed a brāhmana who is free from anger, dutiful, virtuous, without appetites, who is subdued and has received his last body.

Him I call indeed a brāhmana who does not cling to sensual pleasures, like water on a lotus leaf, like a mustard seed on the point of a needle.

Him I call indeed a brāhmana who, even here, knows the end of his own suffering, has put down his burden and is unshackled.

Him I call indeed a brāhmana whose knowledge is deep, who possesses wisdom, who knows the right way and the wrong, and has attained the highest end.

Him I call indeed a brāhmana who keeps aloof both from laymen and from mendicants, who frequents no houses, and has but few desires.

Him I call indeed a brāhmana who without hurting any creatures, whether feeble or strong, does not kill nor cause slaughter.

Him I call indeed a brāhmana who is tolerant with the intolerant, mild with the violent, and free from greed among the greedy.

Him I call indeed a brāhmana from whom anger and hatred, pride and hypocrisy have dropped like a mustard seed from the point of a needle.

Him I call indeed a brāhmana who utters true speech, instructive and free from harshness, so that he offend no one.

Him I call indeed a brāhmana who takes nothing in the world that is not given him, be it long or short, small or large, good or bad.

Him I call indeed a brāhmana who fosters no desires for this world or for the next, has no inclinations and is unshackled.

Him I call indeed a brāhmana who has no interests, and when he has understood the truth, does not say How, how? and who has reached the depth of the Immortal.

Him I call indeed a brāhmana who in this world has risen above both ties, good and evil, who is free from grief, from sin, and from impurity.

Him I call indeed a brāhmana who is bright like the moon, pure, serene, undisturbed, and in whom all gayety is extinct.

Him I call indeed a brāhmana who has traversed this miry road, the impassible world, difficult to pass, and its vanity, who has gone through and reached the other shore, is thoughtful, steadfast, free from doubts, free from attachment, and content.

Him I call indeed a brāhmana who in this world, having abandoned all desires, travels about without a home, and in whom all concupiscence is extinct.

Him I call indeed a brāhmana who, having abandoned all longings, travels about without a home, and in whom all covetousness is extinct.

Him I call indeed a brāhmana who, after leaving all bondage to men, has risen above all bondage to the gods, and is free from all and every bondage.

Him I call indeed a brāhmana who has left what gives pleasure and what gives pain, who is cold and free from all germs of renewed life—the hero who has conquered all the worlds.

Him I call indeed a brāhmana who knows the destruction and the return of beings everywhere, who is free from bondage, welfaring (Sugata), and awakened (Buddha).

Him I call indeed a brāhmana whose path the gods do not know, nor spirits (gandharvas), nor men, whose passions are extinct, and who is an arhat.

Him I call indeed a brāhmana who calls nothing his own, whether it be before, behind, or between; who is poor and free from the love of the world.

Him I call indeed a brāhmana, the manly, the noble, the hero, the great sage, the conqueror, the indifferent, the accomplished, the awakened.

Him I call indeed a brāhmana who knows his former abodes, who sees heaven and hell, has reached the end of births, is perfect in knowledge, a sage, and whose perfections are all perfect.

XX

THE WISE DO NOT GRIEVE

Buddhist literature is rich in parables designed to convey truth in the form of story. Among these the following tale of Kisā Gotamī is outstanding in universal appeal.[7] *It did not necessarily originate with Buddha, but it shows an application of his teaching everyone can understand. Death is an aspect of universal transience. The wise know how to accept its appearing.*

Gotamī was her family name, but because she tired easily, she was called Kisā Gotamī, or Frail Gotamī. She was reborn at Sāvatthi in a poverty-stricken house. When she grew up, she married, going to the house of her husband's family to live. There, because she was the daughter of a poverty-stricken house, they treated her with contempt. After a time she gave birth to a son. Then they accorded her respect.

But when that boy of hers was old enough to play and run hither and about, he died. Sorrow sprang up within her. Thought she: Since the birth of my son, I, who was once denied honor and respect in this very house, have received respect. These folk may even seek to cast my son away. Taking her son on her hip, she went about from one house door to another, saying: "Give me medicine for my son!"

Wherever people encountered her, they said, Where did you ever meet with medicine for the dead? So saying, they clapped their hands and laughed in derision. She had not the slightest idea what they meant.

Now a certain wise man saw her and thought: This woman must have been driven out of her mind by sorrow for her son. But medicine for her, no one else is likely to know—the Possessor of the Ten Forces alone is likely to know. Said he: "Woman, as for medicine for your son—there is no one else who knows—the Possessor of the Ten Forces, the foremost individual in the world

[7] Anguttara Commentary 225-227. Tr. by Eugene Watson Burlingame, in his *Buddhist Parables*, pp. 92-94.

of men and the worlds of the gods, resides at a neighboring monastery. Go to him and ask."

The man speaks the truth, thought she. Taking her son on her hip, when the Tathāgata sat down in the Seat of the Buddhas, she took her stand in the outer circle of the congregation and said: "O Exalted One, give me medicine for my son!"

The Teacher, seeing that she was ripe for conversion, said: "You did well, Gotamī, in coming hither for medicine. Go enter the city, make the rounds of the entire city, beginning at the beginning, and in whatever house no one has ever died, from that house fetch tiny grains of mustard seed."

"Very well, reverend sir," said she. Delighted in heart, she entered within the city, and at the very first house said: "The Possessor of the Ten Forces bids me fetch tiny grains of mustard seed for medicine for my son. Give me tiny grains of mustard seed." "Alas! Gotamī," said they, and brought and gave to her.

"This particular seed I cannot take. In this house some one has died!"

"What say you, Gotamī! Here it is impossible to count the dead!"

"Well then, enough! I'll not take it. The Possessor of the Ten Forces did not tell me to take mustard seed from a house where any one has ever died."

In this same way she went to the second house, and to the third. Thought she: In the entire city this alone must be the way! This the Buddha, full of compassion for the welfare of mankind, must have seen! Overcome with emotion, she went outside of the city, carried her son to the burning-ground, and holding him in her arms, said: "Dear little son, I thought that you alone had been overtaken by this thing which men call death. But you are not the only one death has overtaken. This is a law common to all mankind." So saying, she cast her son away in the burning-ground. Then she uttered the following stanza:

> No village law, no law of market town,
> No law of a single house is this—
> Of all the world and all the worlds of gods
> This only is the Law, that all things are impermanent.

Now when she had so said, she went to the Teacher. Said the Teacher to her: "Gotamī, did you get the tiny grains of mustard seed?" "Done, reverend sir, is the business of the mustard seed! Only give me a refuge!" Then the Teacher recited to her the following stanza in the Dhammapada:

> That man who delights in children and cattle,
> That man whose heart adheres thereto,
> Death takes that man and goes his way,
> As sweeps away a mighty flood a sleeping village.

At the conclusion of the stanza, even as she stood there, she became established in the Fruit of Conversion and requested admission to the Order. The Teacher granted her admission to the Order. She thrice made rightwise circuit of the Teacher, bowed to him, and going to the nuns' convent, entered the Order. Later on she made her full profession, and in no very long time, by the practice of meditation, developed Insight. And the Teacher recited to her this apparition-stanza:

> Though one should live a hundred years,
> Not seeing the Region of the Deathless,
> Better were it for one to live a single day,
> The Region of the Deathless seeing.

At the conclusion of the stanza she attained sainthood.

XXI

THE TRUE CONQUEST

A King's Testimony

One of the greatest rulers in the history of India is the Emperor Asoka, who reigned 269–237 B.C. Third King in the Maurya Dynasty (322–185 B.C.), he inherited from his predecessors a vast realm which he rounded off and completed by conquest of the

Kingdom of the Kalingas on the coast of the Bay of Bengal. Coming under influence of Buddhist teachers at just about this time, he suffered a revulsion at the havoc he had wrought and resolved to devote himself henceforth to promotion of the Buddhist way of life, which he called the Law of Piety. Many of his inscriptions, carved in rock and on stone pillars, are still extant. Among these is the following record of his inner change, a document unique among the engraved monuments of kings.[8] It shows also his zeal to spread the faith beyond the borders of India. The conquest took place 261 B.C. The edict was inscribed 256 B.C.

ROCK EDICT XIII

The Kalingas were conquered by his Sacred and Gracious Majesty the King when he had been consecrated eight years. One hundred and fifty thousand persons were thence carried away captive, one hundred thousand were there slain, and many times that number perished.

Directly after the annexation of the Kalingas, began his Sacred Majesty's zealous protection of the Law of Piety, his love of that Law, and his giving instruction in that Law (Dharma). Thus arose His Sacred Majesty's remorse for having conquered the Kalingas, because the conquest of a country previously unconquered involves the slaughter, death, and carrying away captive of the people. That is a matter of profound sorrow and regret to His Sacred Majesty.

There is, however, another reason for His Sacred Majesty feeling still more regret, inasmuch as in such a country dwell brāhmans or ascetics, or men of various denominations, or householders, upon whom is laid this duty of hearkening to superiors, hearkening to father and mother, hearkening to teachers, and proper treatment of friends, acquaintances, comrades, relatives, slaves, and servants, with fidelity of attachment. To such people in such a country befalls violence, or slaughter, or separation from their loved ones. Or misfortune befalls the friends, acquaintances, comrades,

[8] Tr. by Vincent A. Smith, in his *Asoka, the Buddhist Emperor of India*, pp. 172-175.

and relatives of those who are themselves well protected, while their affection is undiminished. Thus for them also that is a mode of violence. All these several happenings to men are matter of regret to His Sacred Majesty, because it is never the case that people have not faith in some one denomination or other.

Thus of all the people who were then slain, done to death, or carried away captive in the Kalingas, if the hundredth or the thousandth part were to suffer the same fate, it would now be matter of regret to His Sacred Majesty. Moreover, should anyone do him wrong, that too must be borne with by His Sacred Majesty, if it can possibly be borne with. Even upon the forest folk in his dominions His Sacred Majesty looks kindly and he seeks their conversion, for (if he did not) repentance would come upon His Sacred Majesty. They are bidden to turn from evil ways, that they be not chastised. For His Sacred Majesty desires that all animate beings should have security, self-control, peace of mind, and joyousness.

And this is the chiefest conquest in the opinion of His Sacred Majesty—the conquest by the Law of Piety—and this, again, has been won by His Sacred Majesty both in his own dominions and in all the neighboring realms as far as six hundred leagues—where the Greek (Yona) King named Antiochos dwells, and north of that Antiochos to where dwell the four kings,[9] severally named Ptolemy, Antigonos, Magas, and Alexander; and in the south the (realms of the) Cholas and Pāndyas, with Ceylon likewise—and here too, in the King's dominions, among the Yonas, and Kāmbojas, among the Nābhapamtis of Nābhaka, among the Bhojas and Pitinikas, among the Andhras and Pulindas,[10] everywhere

---

[9] These are Antiochos Theos (261-246 B.C.), King of Syria and Western Asia; Ptolemy Philadelphos of Egypt (285-247 B.C.); Antigonos Gonatas of Macedonia (277-239 B.C.); Magas, of Cyrene to the west of Egypt (died 258 B.C.); Alexander of Epirus (272-?258 B.C.).

[10] The foregoing are names of peoples or nations in the more distant regions of Asoka's India. Vincent Smith has described them as "various more or less civilized tribes occupying the slopes of the Himalaya, the regions beyond the Indus, and parts of the Deccan and Central India, which were under imperial control, although not included in the settled provinces administered by the emperor or his viceroys."

men follow His Sacred Majesty's instruction in the Law of Piety. Even where the envoys of His Sacred Majesty do not penetrate, there too men hearing His Sacred Majesty's ordinance based on the Law of Piety and his instruction in that Law, practice and will practice the Law.

And, again, the conquest thereby won everywhere is everywhere a conquest full of delight. Delight is found in the conquests made by the Law. That delight, however, is only a small matter. His Sacred Majesty regards as bearing much fruit only that which concerns the other world.

And for this purpose has this pious edict been written in order that my sons and grandsons, who may be, should not regard it as their duty to conquer a new conquest. If, perchance, they become engaged in a conquest by arms, they should take pleasure in patience and gentleness, and regard as (the only true) conquest the conquest won by piety. That avails for both this world and the next. Let all joy be in effort, because that avails for both this world and the next.

PART THREE
SANSKRIT AND CHINESE BUDDHIST LITERATURE

XXII

THE BODHISATTVA IDEAL

The literature of Far Eastern Buddhism belongs to a form of the religion which is different from that of Southern Asia as represented by the Pāli texts. It reflects a development which took place in Indian Buddhism from about the beginning of the Christian Era. Written chiefly in Sanskrit, most of the literature of this development (Mahāyāna Buddhism) was later translated into Chinese and Tibetan. Here the highest religious life is conceived as one lived in the spirit of a Bodhisattva, i.e., one who, like Buddha before his Enlightenment, out of deep compassion aspires and strives after perfect enlightenment in order to save all living beings from ignorance, error and suffering. On the way to this goal of becoming a Buddha for the sake of others such a person cultivates all the virtues through innumerable lives of unselfish devotion. The following description [1] *of the qualities of Bodhisattvas as given in a noted Sanskrit text portrays this new ideal of the good life.*[2]

They are Bodhisattvas who live on from life to life in the possession of manifold good qualities. They are Bodhisattvas who have won the mastery over karma, and made their deeds renowned through their accumulation of merit. They are resolute and valiant, intent on endurance, trustworthy, upright and sincere. They are generous, firm, gentle, tender, patient, whole and tranquil of heart, difficult to overcome and defeat, intent on what is real, charitable,

[1] Mahāvastu, I, 133-134. Tr. by J. J. Jones from the Buddhist Sanskrit, in *Sacred Books of the Buddhists,* Vol. XVI, 1, pp. 105-106.
[2] This and the following selection are drawn from a Sanskrit work which is not a Mahāyāna text in the strict sense. The ideas of the Buddhas and Bodhisattvas expressed in the work, however, contain in germ conceptions which were greatly expanded and universalised in the Mahāyāna faith of the Far East.

and faithful to their promises. They are intelligent, brilliantly intelligent, gifted with insight, and not given to gratification of sensual desires. They are devoted to the highest good. They win converts by the (four) means of sympathetic appeal. They are pure in conduct and clean of heart, full of exceeding great veneration, full of civility to elder and noble. They are resourceful, in all matters using conciliatory and agreeable methods, and in affairs of government they are adept in persuasive speech. They are men whose voice is not checked in the assembly, men who pour forth their eloquence in a mighty stream. With knowledge as their banner they are skilled in drawing the multitude to them. They are endowed with equanimity, and their means of living is beyond reproach. They are men of successful achievements, and are ready to come to the assistance of others and help those in distress. They do not become enervated by prosperity, and do not lose composure in adversity. They are skilled in uprooting the vices of mean men. They are unwearying in clothing the nakedness of others. They are anxious not to blight the maturing of their karma, and they acquire the roots of virtue by keeping themselves aloof from passion, hatred and folly. They are skilled in bringing solace to those in trouble and misfortune. They do not hesitate to render all kinds of service. In all matters they are untiring in their purpose. They are endowed here in this world with the profound attributes of a Buddha. In their progress toward their goal they are undefiled in acts of body, speech and thought. Through the uprightness of their lives in former existences they are untarnished and pure in conduct. Possessing perfect knowledge they are men of undimmed understanding. They are eager to win the sphere of power of a Buddha—so far are they from refusing it. With knowledge as their banner they are untiring in speech and skilled in teaching. Being of irreproachable character they are immune from disaster. They are free from sin. They shun the threefold distractions. Leaving vain babblers alone, they love their enemies. They do not indulge in sexual pleasures. They know how to win the affection of all creatures. When they enter the world they become endowed with powers that are in accordance with the vow they have made. In all matters they are skilled in the knowledge of correct and faulty conclusions. They are rich in goodness and blessed with good qualities. Eminent, wise in their illimitable virtue, they are serene among their fellows. On this matter it is said:

As it is not possible for any bird to reach the confines of the sky, so it is not possible for any man to comprehend the good qualities of the self-becoming Buddhas.

XXIII

IN PRAISE OF THE BUDDHAS

In Mahāyāna Buddhism the great achievement following upon the career of a Bodhisattva is to become a Buddha, a perfectly enlightened, compassionate saviour of all suffering beings. Conceived as appearing in the world though transcending it, these exalted attainers of all excellence are hymned with endless praise in the scriptures. Scholastically there is ascribed to them possession of thirty-two marks of a Great Man, eighty minor characteristics, eighteen special attributes, ten powers, etc. The following selection[3] *gives an informal description of their quality. In the Far East, Buddhahood is thought of as an ultimate goal for every good Buddhist, however many rebirths its pursuit entails.*

Perfect Buddhas, my pious friend, are ready to serve; are able to perceive the right occasion; have clear insight; discern the high and the low; are good at the beginning and at the end; raise the banner of Dharma, the invincible banner; are eager in fight and combat; are eloquent; know what is deathless, and on occasion practice charity at the cost of their lives. They urge on the blind, and rebuke those who go along devious ways.

[3] Mahāvastu 176-177. Tr. by J. J. Jones, in *Sacred Books of the Buddhists*, Vol. XVI, 1, 139-140. (Cf. note 2 on p. 107.)

On this matter it is said:

> Altogether perfect in qualities, intent on all things that are salutary, leaders and saviours that they are, all the Buddhas are praised by wise men.
>
> With unconfused knowledge, with pure mind, they shine in the three worlds like the full moon in the sky.
>
> Instinct with perfect virtue, they are leaders of men by their pleasing and lovely conduct. They raise a great shout.
>
> The heroes, bent on rendering service, instruct men, and with an insight into truth quell the strife of others.
>
> The best of men, though born into the world, are not besmirched by it. The lords, profound in their attributes, are beyond description.
>
> Having shouldered their heavy yoke, the wise ones do not falter, but, suiting actions to their words, they are of irreproachable conduct.
>
> With fire of knowledge the lords burn the noxious poisonous weed of false belief, and without fear or trembling they hold out to men the prospect of the beyond.
>
> The valiant men, having traversed the wilderness and attained peace, in their wisdom proclaim: "Here is the place where no terror is.
>
> "Here is found no recurrence of old age and death and disease. Here is experienced no event of tribulation or sorrow."
>
> Devas and men, hearing his sweet words and paying due heed to them, attain to that well-being.
>
> Therefore their renown is spread far and wide and is supreme in the three worlds. The Buddhas fare onward, praised of good men, and never do they rest.

XXIV

BUDDHIST PROVERBS

In Mahāyāna tradition, there is a belief that everyone is potentially a Buddha. Gotama is regarded as only one of many Buddhas who have appeared in this and other worlds. Of these latter the greatest is the Buddha Amitabha who reigns in a paradise situated in the western quarter of the universe. Anyone who calls upon his name in faith will be reborn in his "Western Heaven." Further, any saint who takes a vow to become a Buddha is called a bodhisattva and is regarded as accumulating, by multiplied good deeds through many successive lives, a store of merit available to all who trust him. Among the great bodhisattvas is Kuan-yin, the Goddess of Mercy. She is on the way to become a fully enlightened Buddha, but meantime is a great saviour and helper of human beings. Amitabha and Kuan-yin are really compassionate deities much invoked in China and Japan. In the following popular proverbs [4] *such devotional beliefs are taken for granted.*

> The truth of Buddha is infinite; the door of truth is wide open.
> Without suffering one cannot become a Buddha.
> The mind of a child is the mind of a Buddha.
> When you pray, pray to one Buddha only.
> When all is well, one neglects to burn incense; when in pressing need, one embraces the Buddha's feet.
> The foundation of Buddhism is Compassion; its door is Convenience.
> In every home there is a Goddess of Mercy; in every place there is an Amitabha Buddha.
> First extinguish the fire in your heart, then light the lamp before the Buddha.
> Wherefore light a lamp if the mind is not enlightened; wherefore recite a sūtra if the mind is not fair?
> Provide conveniences to others at all times; accumulate merits of all kinds.

[4] Tr. by Shao Chang Lee, in his *Popular Buddhism in China*, pp. 21-22.

To save one human life is better than to build a seven-storied pagoda.
To do one good deed is better than to construct a nine-storied pagoda.
Better bestow blessings nearby than burn incense afar.
Each receives in accordance with what he cultivates.
Merit is never in vain.
Hundred years elapse accompanying a mere change; myriad things become void at the turning of the head.
Man dies even as a lamp goes out.
The bright moon is not always round; the multicolored clouds are easily scattered.
Man ferries over life even as a traveler ferries over the sea.
The ancients did not see the moon of the present; the present moon did once shine upon the ancients.
Close your eyes: your ego and other beings are all void.
Beauty does not delude man to folly; it is man who deludes himself to folly.
As long as one is a monk for a day, he will apply the baton to the bell for a day.
Abstinence from eating and killing [animate creatures] is already a Bodhisattvahood [in becoming].
Before a genuine Bodhisattva, do not burn counterfeit incense.
A mind enlightened is heaven; a mind darkened is hell.
Cultivate in this life merits of the life of the future.
To know the causes emerging from the previous life, look at your present lot; to know the causes affecting the future life, look at your present deeds.
He who preaches the Truth expounds the doctrine of emptiness and nothingness for the benefit not only of other living beings, but also for the self.
He who sees through superficialities regards death and life as so much sorrow while lingering, and so much freedom after quitting.
The mind is really nothingness. Leave defamations and frowns alone. Both are easy to tolerate.
Worldly involvements should be light—even if there were only

vegetarian diet and limpid water, to enjoy these should it be at all difficult?

[Some people possess] the mouth of a Buddha but the heart of a serpent.

The human mind makes mischiefs, like a monkey; human consciousness gallops like a horse.

XXV

ESSENCE OF THE WISDOM SŪTRA

In one of its philosophical systems, Mahāyāna Buddhism teaches that Supreme or Transcendent Truth lies beyond the grasp of either sense perception or conception. From the standpoint of our ordinary experience and thought it is "empty." Conversely, measured by the Supreme Truth all objects and events as apprehended in the distinctions of sense and thought (even of the loftiest ideas) are also "empty." Perfect wisdom, therefore, consists in realizing ultimate truth as "The Void" (Śūnya), which does not mean unreality, but that which is beyond all powers of discrimination. Attaining realization of The Void is "to reach the Other Shore." The literature of this philosophy is extensive, but the following selection [5] gives a condensation of its essential ideas. By devout Buddhists in China this little Scripture is frequently recited. The formula at the end is considered very efficacious.

When Bodhisattva Avalokiteśvara [6] was meditating deeply on the "Perfect Wisdom by means of which one reaches the Other Shore," he perceived clearly that the "five constituents of being"

[5] From Hsüan Ts'ang's version of the Prajñā-pāramitā Hridaya Sūtra. Tr. by Shao Chang Lee, *op. cit.*, pp. 23-26.
[6] Avalokiteśvara is the Sanskrit name of the deity of mercy, in Chinese Kuan-yin, in Japanese Kwannon, generally known as the "Goddess of Mercy."

are all Śūnya, and so was saved from all kinds of suffering and misery.

[Then he addressed himself to Sariputra, saying:] "O Sariputra! Matter is not different from Śūnya and Śūnya is not different from matter. Matter is Śūnya and Śūnya is matter.

"O Sariputra! All things are Śūnya. They neither come into existence nor pass out of existence. They neither defile nor purify. They neither increase nor decrease.

"Therefore in Śūnya there is no form, no sensation, no idea, no will, no consciousness. There is no eye, no ear, no nose, no tongue, no body, no thought, and so there is no color, no sound, no odor, no taste, no contact, no mental object.

"There is neither world of vision nor world of thought and consciousness. There is neither ignorance nor termination of ignorance. There is neither old age and death nor termination of old age and death.

"There is neither suffering, nor cause of suffering, nor extinction of suffering, nor way of escape from suffering.

"There is neither knowledge nor attainment in knowledge.

"Because there is no attainment in knowledge, the Bodhisattvas rely on the 'Perfect Wisdom by means of which one reaches the Other Shore.' [Because they rely on the Perfect Wisdom] their minds are freed from hindrances and obstructions.

"Because they are freed from hindrances and obstructions, they have neither fear nor dread, and they do away entirely with perverted, perverse, dreamy thoughts, and finally reach Nirvāṇa.

"The Buddhas of the past, present, and future, by relying on the 'Perfect Wisdom by means of which one reaches the Other Shore,' attain the 'Highest State of Enlightenment.' "

So we know that the "Perfect Wisdom by means of which one reaches the Other Shore" is a great divine formula, a great enlightening formula, an unsurpassed formula, an unequaled formula, which can remove all kinds of suffering.

This is true and real, and therefore we make known the formula on the "Perfect Wisdom by means of which one reaches the Other Shore."

The formula is said thus:

> Ferry, ferry, ferry over to the Other Shore!
> Ferry all beings over to the Other Shore!
> Perfect Wisdom! Hail!

XXVI

CONCLUSION OF THE DIAMOND SŪTRA

One of the most popular scriptures in China, Korea, and Japan is the Diamond Sūtra. Like the Essence of the Wisdom Sūtra, its underlying doctrine is a <u>denial of the reality of the phenomenal world</u>. With more illustrations and references to familiar beliefs, however, it builds up its thesis cumulatively, negating every particular way of perceiving, thinking and talking about characteristics of things and events. It reiterates throughout that these distinctions, even when taught by the Buddha himself, are only assigned characteristics and names, not to be taken as ultimate truth which inexpressibly transcends them. They are transient appearances. Therefore, he who would become enlightened must learn not to depend upon them.

Although ultimate truth is beyond comprehension, the reward for the believer is also beyond comprehension. Accordingly a measureless efficacy is ascribed to recitation of the words of this scripture in devout faith. For its requirement is not comprehension of its highest meaning, but childlike trust that it is there. This is doubtless the reason for the great popularity of this scripture with the laity.

The two chapters here given are typical of the whole.[7] In them Buddha instructs his disciple Subhuti.

[7] From Kumārajīva's Chinese version of the Vajracchedikā. Tr. by Shao Chang Lee, *op. cit.*, pp. 51-52.

XXXI

"Subhuti, if a man says that Buddha preaches the doctrine of the reality of the existence of the ego, of man, and of all beings and personalities, do you think that man really understands the meaning of my discourse?"

"No, O World-honored One. That man does not understand the meaning of your discourse. And why? Because the World-honored One says, The reality of the existence of the ego, of man, and of all beings and personalities is not the reality of the existence of the ego, of man, and of all beings and personalities, but is merely considered as the 'reality of the existence of the ego, of man, and of all beings and personalities.'"

Buddha rejoined: "Subhuti, he who resolves to attain the Highest State of Enlightenment should thus understand, thus perceive, and thus believe and explain: All things are being unborn. O Subhuti, what are regarded as characteristics of things are considered by Tathāgata as 'non-characteristics of things' and are merely named 'characteristics of things.'"

XXXII

"Subhuti, if good men and good women, who resolve to become enlightened, would take this Sūtra, even a four-line gāthā, and study it and explain it to others, their merit would be much greater than the man who used for almsgiving the seven treasures that would fill the innumerable worlds. How should they explain this Sūtra to others? They should not depend on the characteristics of things. They should be natural and firm in their conviction. And why? Because

> All activities
> Should be looked upon merely as being like a dream,
> A phantasm, a bubble, a shadow,
> A drop of dew, or a flash of lightning."

Thus Buddha concluded his discourse on this Sūtra. Upon hearing what Buddha had said, the venerable Subhuti, the monks, nuns, lay men and women, and all beings in the worlds of the gods and men and of the terrestrial spirits rejoiced exceedingly. They believed in it, accepted it, and reverently put it into practice.

XXVII

THE PRODIGAL SON AND THE SEEKING FATHER

In Mahāyāna Buddhism the earthly Gotama or Śākyamuni Buddha recedes into the background. He is regarded as one expression only of a more ultimate and profound Being. That Being is the Eternal Buddha who, through all enlightened ones in all ages and places, is forever seeking to reveal himself up to the measure of each individual's capacity to understand. In the Lotus Scripture, greatly revered in China and Japan, this Eternal Buddha is called "The Father of All Worlds," who is portrayed as everlastingly seeking to bring his sons out from the realm of ignorance and sorrow into the boundless riches of perfect enlightenment. This scripture is a masterpiece of apocalyptic vision and imagery, reminding us of the Revelation to John in our Christian Bible. In the Chinese version of Kumārajīva, from which the following selection is translated,[8] the literary quality is of the highest.

It is like a youth who, on attaining manhood, leaves his father and runs away. For long he dwells in some other country, ten, twenty, or fifty years. The older he grows, the more needy he becomes. Roaming about in all directions to seek clothing and food, he gradually wanders along till he unexpectedly approaches his native country. From the first the father searched for his son,

[8] From Miao-fa-lien-hua-ching. Tr. by W. E. Soothill, as *The Lotus of the Wonderful Law*, pp. 106-113. (The Chinese version itself is a translation from the Sanskrit Saddharma Pundarīka Sūtra.)

but in vain, and meanwhile has settled in a certain city. His home becomes very rich; his goods and treasures are incalculable; gold, silver, lapis lazuli, corals, amber, crystal, and other gems so increase that his treasuries overflow; many youths and slaves has he, retainers and attendants, and countless elephants, horses, carriages, animals to ride, and kine and sheep. His revenues and investments spread to other countries, and his traders and customers are many in the extreme.

At this time, the poor son, wandering through village after village, and passing through countries and cities, at last reaches the city where his father has settled. Always has the father been thinking of his son, yet, though he has been parted from him over fifty years, he has never spoken of the matter to anyone, only pondering over it within himself and cherishing regret in his heart, as he reflects: Old and worn, I own much wealth; gold, silver, and jewels, granaries and treasuries overflowing; but I have no son. Some day my end will come and my wealth be scattered and lost, for there is no one to whom I can leave it. Thus does he often think of his son, and earnestly repeats this reflection: If I could only get back my son and commit my wealth to him, how contented and happy should I be, with never a further anxiety!

World-honored One! Meanwhile the poor son, hired for wages here and there, unexpectedly arrives at his father's house. Standing by the gate, he sees from afar his father seated on a lion-couch, his feet on a jeweled footstool, revered and surrounded by brāhmanas, kshatriyas, and citizens, and with strings of pearls, worth thousands and myriads, adorning his body; attendants and young slaves with white chowries wait upon him right and left; he is covered by a rich canopy from which hang streamers of flowers; perfume is sprinkled on the earth, all kinds of famous flowers are scattered around, and precious things are placed in rows for his acceptance or rejection. Such is his glory, and the honor of his dignity. The poor son, seeing his father possessed of such great power, is seized with fear, regretting that he has come to this place, and secretly reflects thus: This must be a king, or someone of royal rank; it is no place for me to obtain anything for the hire of my labor. I had better go to some poor hamlet, where there is a place for letting out my labor, and food and clothing are easier to get. If I tarry here long, I may suffer oppression and forced service.

Having reflected thus, he hastens away. Meanwhile, the rich elder on his lion-seat has recognized his son at first sight, and with great joy in his heart has also reflected: Now I have someone to whom my treasuries of wealth are to be made over. Always have I been thinking of this my son, with no means of seeing him; but suddenly he himself has come and my longing is satisfied. Though worn with years, I yearn for him as of old.

Instantly he dispatches his attendants to pursue him quickly and fetch him back. Thereupon the messengers hasten forth to seize him. The poor son, surprised and scared, loudly cries his complaint: "I have committed no offense against you; why should I be arrested?" The messengers all the more hasten to lay hold of him and compel him to go back. Thereupon the poor son, thinking within himself that though he is innocent yet he will be imprisoned, and that now he will surely die, is all the more terrified, faints away and falls prostrate on the ground. The father, seeing this from afar, sends word to the messengers: "I have no need for this man. Do not bring him by force. Sprinkle cold water on his face to restore him to consciousness and do not speak to him any further." Wherefore? The father, knowing that his son's disposition is inferior, knowing that his own lordly position has caused distress to his son, yet convinced that he is his son, tactfully does not say to others: "This is my son."

A messenger says to the son: "I now set you free; go wherever you will." The poor son is delighted, thus obtaining the unexpected. He rises from the ground and goes to a poor hamlet in search of food and clothing. Then the elder, desiring to attract his son, sets up a device. Secretly he sends two men, doleful and shabby in appearance, saying: "You go and visit that place and gently say to the poor man, There is a place for you to work here; you will be given double wages. If the poor man agrees, bring him back and give him work. If he asks what work you wish him to do, then you may say to him, We will hire you for scavenging, and we both also will work along with you." Then the two messengers go in search of the poor son and, having found him, place before him the above proposal. Thereupon the poor son, having received his wages beforehand, joins with them in removing a dirt heap.

His father, beholding the son, is struck with compassion for, and wonder at, him. Another day he sees at a distance, through a window, his son's figure, gaunt, lean, and doleful, filthy and unclean with dirt and dust; thereupon he takes off his strings of jewels, his soft attire, and ornaments, and puts on a coarse, torn, and dirty garment, smears his body with dust, takes a dust hod in his right hand, and with an appearance fear-inspiring says to the laborers: "Get on with your work, don't be lazy." By such a device he gets near to his son, to whom he afterward says: "Ay, my man, you stay and work here, do not go again elsewhere; I will increase your wages; give whatever you need, bowls, utensils, rice, wheat, flour, salt, vinegar and so on; have no hesitation; besides there is an old and worn-out servant whom you shall be given if you need him. Be at ease in your mind; I am, as it were, your father; do not be worried again. Wherefore? I am old and advanced in years, but you are young and vigorous; all the time you have been working, you have never been deceitful, lazy, angry or grumbling; I have never seen you, like the other laborers, with such vices as these. From this time forth you shall be as my own begotten son."

Thereupon the elder gives him a new name and calls him a son. The poor son, though he rejoices at this happening, still thinks of himself as a humble hireling. For this reason, during twenty years he continues to be employed in scavenging. After this period, there grows mutual confidence between them, and he goes in and out and is at his ease, though his abode is still the original place.

World-honored One! Then the elder becomes ill and, knowing that he will die before long, says to the poor son: "Now I possess abundance of gold, silver, and precious things, and my granaries and treasuries are full to overflowing. The quantities of these things, and the amounts which should be received and given, I want you to understand in detail. Such is my mind, and you must agree to this my wish. Wherefore? Because, now, I and you are of the same mind. Be increasingly careful so that there be no waste."

The poor son accepts his instruction and commands, and becomes acquainted with all the goods, gold, silver, and precious things, as well as all the granaries and treasuries, but has no idea of expecting to inherit so much as a meal, while his abode is still the original place and he is yet unable to abandon his sense of inferiority.

After a short time has again passed, the father, knowing that his son's ideas have gradually been enlarged, his aspirations developed, and that he despises his previous state of mind, on seeing that his own end is approaching, commands his son to come, and gathers together his relatives, and the kings, ministers, kshatriyas, and citizens. When they are all assembled, he thereupon addresses them saying: "Now, gentlemen, this is my son, begotten by me. It is over fifty years since, from a certain city, he left me and ran away to endure loneliness and misery. His former name was so-and-so and my name was so-and-so. At that time in that city I sought him sorrowfully. Suddenly in this place I met and regained him. This is really my son and I am really his father. Now all the wealth which I possess entirely belongs to my son, and all my previous disbursements and receipts are known by this son."

World-honored One! When the poor son heard these words of his father, great was his joy at such unexpected news, and thus he thought: Without any mind for, or effort on my part, these treasures now come of themselves to me.

World-honored One! The very rich elder is the Tathāgata, and we are all as the Buddha's sons. The Tathāgata has always declared that we are his sons. World-honored One! Because of the three sufferings, in the midst of births and deaths we have borne all kinds of torments, being deluded and ignorant and enjoying our attachment to trifles. Today the World-honored One has caused us to ponder over and remove the dirt of all diverting discussions of inferior things. In these we have hitherto been diligent to make progress and have got, as it were, a day's pay for our effort to reach Nirvāṇa. Obtaining this, we greatly rejoiced and were contented, saying to ourselves: For our diligence and progress in the Buddha-law what we have received is ample. But the World-honored One, knowing beforehand that our minds were attached to low desires and took delight in inferior things, let us go our own way and did not discriminate for us, saying: You shall yet have possession of the treasury of Tathāgata-knowledge. The World-honored One, in his tactfulness, told of the Tathāgata-wisdom; but we, though following the Buddha and receiving a day's wage of Nirvāṇa, deemed this a sufficient gain, never having a mind to seek after the Great Vehicle. We also have declared and expounded the Tathāgata-wisdom to bodhisattvas, but in regard to this Great Vehicle we have never had a longing for it. Wherefore? The Buddha, knowing that our minds delighted in inferior things, by his tactfulness taught according to our capacity, but still we did not perceive that we were really Buddha-sons.

Now we have just realized that the World-honored One does not grudge even the Buddha-wisdom. Wherefore? From of old we are really sons of Buddha, but have only taken pleasure in minor matters; if we had had a mind to take pleasure in tne Great, the Buddha would have preached the Great Vehicle Law to us. At length, in this Sūtra, he preaches only the One Vehicle; and though formerly, in the presence of bodhisattvas, he spoke disparagingly of śrāvakas who were pleased with minor matters, yet the Buddha had in reality been instructing them in the Great Vehicle. Therefore we say that though we had no mind to hope or expect it, yet now the Great Treasure of the King of the Law has of itself come to us, and such things as Buddha-sons should obtain we have all obtained.

XXVIII

BUDDHA THE LIFE-GIVING RAIN CLOUD

Again from the Lotus Scripture,[9] we have in the following a poetical portrayal of the all-sufficiency of the Eternal Buddha, appearing in the world to bring life, and refreshing to gods and men and

[9] W. E. Soothill, *op. cit.*, p. 127.

every living creature. The all-enriching rain is the Law which he teaches.

> In like manner also the Buddha
> Appears here in the world,
> Like unto a great cloud
> Universally covering all things;
> And having appeared in the world,
> He, for the sake of the living,
> Discriminates and proclaims
> The truth in regard to all laws.
> The Great Holy World-honored One,
> Among the gods and men
> And among the other beings,
> Proclaims abroad this word:
> I am the Tathāgata,
> The Most Honored among men;
> I appear in the world
> Like unto this great cloud,
> To pour enrichment on all
> Parched living beings,
> To free them from their misery,
> To attain the joy of peace,
> Joy of the present world,
> And joy of Nirvāṇa.
> Gods, men, and everyone!
> Hearken well with your mind—
> Come you here to me,
> Behold the Peerless Honored One!
> I am the World-honored,
> Who cannot be equaled.
> To give rest to every creature,
> I appear in the world,
> And, to the hosts of the living,
> Preach the Pure Law, sweet as dew.

BUDDHISM

XXIX

THE WHITE LOTUS ODE

In the following poem [10] the theme is the "Pure Land" or "Western Paradise" of the great heavenly Buddha Amitabha. According to sacred legend Amitabha, from great compassion and by accumulated merit, established this paradise as a realm into which all who call upon his name in faith will be saved after death. In the Pure Land Sects of China and Japan, yearning adoration is directed toward Amitabha and his paradise in impressive hymns and devotional poetry. The "White Lotus Ode" by Hui Yüan, in particular, reminds the Western reader of "Jerusalem the Golden," by Bernard of Cluny.

What words can picture the beauty and breadth
Of that pure and glistening land?
That land where the blossoms ne'er wither from age,
Where the golden gates gleam like purest water—
The land that rises in terrace on terrace
Of diamond-clad steps and shining jade—
That land where there are none but fragrant bowers,
Where the Utpala lotus unfolds itself freely.
O hear the sweet tones from hillside and grove
The All-Father's praise from the throats of the birds!

And the ages fly by in an endless chain,
Never broken by summer's or winter's change.
The burning sun can never more frighten.
The icy storms' power long ago is subdued.
The clouds full of light and the green mantled forests
Now cradle all things in their endless peace.
Now the soul is set free from the haunts of darkness
And rests secure in the dwelling of truth.
See, all that was dim and beclouded on earth
Here is revealed, appropriated, secured.

[10] In Karl Ludvig Reichelt, *Truth and Tradition in Chinese Buddhism*, pp. 136-137.

There ne'er was a country so brightened with gladness
As the Land of the Pure there far off to the West.
There stands Amitabha with shining adornments,
He makes all things ready for the Eternal Feast.
He draws every burdened soul up from the depths
And lifts them up into his peaceful abode.
The great transformation is accomplished for the worm
Who is freed from the body's oppressive sorrows.
It receives as a gift a spiritual body,
A body which shines in the sea of spirits.

And who indeed is it with grace in his tones,
Who sends his smile out to the dwellings of the suffering,
And who indeed is it whose glance is like the sun
Who shows his compassion on life and is victor?
Yes, it is God himself, who sits on the throne
And by his Law, redeems from all need.
With gold-adorned arm, with crown of bright jewels,
With power over sin, over grief, over death.
None other is like to our God in his greatness,
And none can requite his compassion's great power!

The following little verse from "Masses for the Dead" is of special beauty. It, also, is addressed to Amitabha.

"Thou perfect master,
  Who shinest upon all things and all men,
  As gleaming moonlight plays upon a thousand waters at the same time!
  Thy great compassion does not pass by a single creature.
  Steadily and quietly sails the great ship of compassion across the sea of sorrow.
  Thou art the Great Physician for a sick and impure world,
  In pity giving the invitation to the Paradise of the West.

XXX

PHILOSOPHICAL IDEALISM

Although the founder of Buddhism did not himself encourage speculative reflection, his followers in India found it not possible to escape philosophical problems of this character in their debates with non-Buddhists. One of the greatest of these later thinkers was Vasubandhu, who, together with his brother Asanga, in the fourth century A.D., formulated a system of metaphysical idealism. The writings of both Asanga and Vasubandhu were translated into Chinese and became the subject of much study and comment in the Far East. In the following extract [11] from Vasubandhu's Treatise in Twenty Stanzas on Representation Only, *as translated from the Chinese version of Hsüan Tsang (661 A.D.) we have some of his reasonings to prove that no world of extra-mental entities exists beyond the realm of consciousness. This idealism he believed was Buddha's inner intention, though not expressed in the early dogma.*

[A questioner has just asked whether there is not a realm of separate, really existing outer elements which are the objects of our several kinds of sense consciousness. Vasubandhu replies:]

The Stanza says:

X

That realm is neither one thing,
    Nor is it many atoms;
    Again, it is not an agglomeration,
Because the atom is not proved.

---

[11] From *Wei Shih Er Shih Lun,* or *The Treatise in Twenty Stanzas on Representation-Only,* by Vasubandhu. (In Sanskrit called *Vijñaptimātratā-siddhi; Vimśatikā.*) Tr. from the Chinese version of Hsüan Tsang by Clarence H. Hamilton. "American Oriental Series," XIII, 43-65.

The complete *Treatise* consists of Twenty Stanzas with accompanying prose commentary, both verse and prose being from Vasubandhu himself. In tne extract here given, Stanzas X-XVI are reprinted, the many footnotes of the translator being omitted.

How can this be said? The meaning is that if there really are external bases of cognition which respectively become objects of sense representation, then such an outer realm must either be one, as in the assertion of the Vaiśesikas that there is form having parts; or it must be many, as in the affirmation that there are very many real atoms which in agglomeration and combination act together as objects. But the external object cannot logically be one, because we cannot grasp the substance of the whole apart from the parts. Also it logically is not many, because we cannot apprehend the atoms separately. Again logically, they do not in agglomeration or combination make objects, because the theory of single real atoms is not proved.

[Question] How can you say it is not proved?

[Answer] The Stanza says:

XI

One atom joined with six others
    Must consist of six parts.
    If it is in the same place with six,
The aggregate must be as one atom.

If one atom on each of its six sides joins with another atom, it must consist of six parts, because the place of one does not permit of being the place of the others. If there are six atoms in one atom's place, then all the aggregates must be as one atom in quantity because, though revolving in mutual confrontation, they do not exceed that quantity; and so aggregates also must be invisible.

[Objection] The Vaibhāsikas of Kaśmir say: The theory that atoms join together is wrong because they do not have spatial divisions—dismiss such an error as the above—but aggregates have the principle of joining together because they do have spatial divisions.

[Answer] This also is not so, for the Stanza says:

XII

> Since it is stated that atoms do not join,
>   Of what then is the joining of the aggregates?
>   If joining is not proved of the latter,
> It is not because they have no spatial divisions.

Now we must examine the principle and tendency of their statement. Since apart from atoms there are no aggregates, and there is no joining of atoms, then of what is the joining of the aggregates? If you change the statement to save your position and say that aggregates also do not join one another, then you should not say that atoms are without combination because of having no spatial divisions. Aggregates have spatial divisions and yet you do not grant their combination. Therefore the noncombining of atoms is not due to their lack of spatial division. For this reason the single real atom is not proved. Whether atomic combination is or is not admitted, the mistake is still as we have said. Whether spatial division of atoms is or is not admitted, both views are greatly in error.

[Question] For what reason?

[Answer] The Stanza says:

XIII

> If the atom has spatial divisions
>   It logically should not make a unity;
>   If it has none, there should be neither
>   shadow nor occultation;
> Aggregates being no different (would likewise be)
>   without these two

If the six spatial divisions of the single atom are different, several parts making up the body, how can unity be proven? If the single atom is without different spatial divisions, then when the light of the rising sun strikes upon it how does a shadow occur on the other side, since there is no other part where the light does not reach? Again, if we assert that atoms are without spatial divisions, how can there be mutual occultation of one by another, since there is no remaining portion of the one to which the other does not go, by which we may speak of mutual obstruction of one by another? Since they do not mutually obstruct, then all the atoms must revolve in the same place; and the quantity of all aggregates is the same as one atom. The error is as we have said above.

[Question] Why not admit that shadow and occultation pertain to aggregates but not to atoms?

[Answer] Can it be that different from the atoms you admit aggregates which cast shadows and cause occultation?

[Objector] Not so!

[Answer] If that is the case, the aggregates must be without these two phenomena. That is, if aggregates are not different from the atoms, then shadow and occultation must not belong to the aggregates. The intelligence analyzes, arranges and distinguishes, but whether it sets up atoms or aggregates, both are unrealities.

[Question] Of what use is it to consider and choose between atoms and aggregates when you still cannot get rid of external sense quality?

[Answer] Here again, what is this quality?

[Objector] I mean that the object of vision is also the real nature of the color green, and so on with all the other sense qualities.

[Answer] We must judge whether this "object of vision, etc." which is the "real nature of green, etc." is one or many.

[Objector] Suppose we say, what is the error?

[Answer] Both views are in error. The fault of multiplicity is as explained before. Unity also is irrational.

The Stanza says:

XIV

> Assuming unity, there must be no walking progressively
>   At one time, no grasping and not grasping,
>   And no plural, disconnected condition;
> Moreover no scarcely perceptible, tiny things.

If there is no separation and difference, and all colored things which the eye can reach are asserted to be one thing, then there can be no reason in walking progressively on the ground, for if one step is taken it reaches everywhere: again there cannot be simultaneously a grasping here and a not grasping there, for the reason that a unitary thing cannot at one time be both obtained and not obtained. A single place, also, ought not to contain disconnected things, such as elephants, horses, etc. If the place contains one, it also contains the rest. How can we say that one is distinguished from another? Granting two things present, how comes it that in one place there can be both occupancy and nonoccupancy, that there can be a seeing of emptiness between? Moreover, there should also be no such scarcely perceptible tiny things as water animalcules, because being in the same single space with the coarse things they should be of equal measure. If you say it is by characteristic aspect that one object differs from another, and that they do not become different things from any other reason, then you certainly must admit that this discriminated thing repeatedly divided becomes many atoms. Now it has already been argued that an atom is not a single real thing. Consequently, apart from consciousness sense organs such as the eye, and sense objects such as color, are all unprovable. From these considerations we best prove the doctrine that only representations exist.

[Question] The existence or nonexistence of anything is determined by means of proof. Among all means of proof immediate perception is the most excellent. If there are no external objects, how is there this awareness of objects such as are now immediately evident to me?

[Answer] This evidence is inadequate, for the Stanza says:

XV

Immediate awareness is the same as in dreams.
   At the time when immediate awareness has arisen,
   Seeing and its object are already nonexistent;
How can it be admitted that perception exists?

Just as in time of dreaming, although there are no outer objects, such immediate awareness may be had, so also must the immediate awareness at other times be understood. Therefore to adduce this as evidence is inadequate. Again, if at a certain time there is this immediate awareness, such as the color now evident to me, at that time along with the object the seeing is already nonexistent: (1) because such awareness necessarily belongs to the discriminative action of the intellective consciousness, and (2) because at that time the visual and other sense consciousness have already faded out. According to those who hold the doctrine of momentariness,[12] at the time when this awareness arises the immediate objects, visible, tangible, audible, etc., are already destroyed. How can you admit that at this time there is immediate perception?

[Objection] But a past immediate experience is required before intellective consciousness can remember; for this reason we decide that there is a previously experienced object. The beholding of this object is what we concede to be immediate perception. From this the doctrine that external objects truly exist is established.

[Answer] If you wish to prove the existence of external objects from "first experiencing, later remembering," this theory also fails.

[Objector] Why so?

[Answer] The Stanza says:

XVI (*First part*)

As has been said, the apparent object
is a representation.
It is from this that memory arises. . . .

As we have said earlier, although there is no external object, a sense representation, visual, etc., appears as an outer object. From this comes the later state with its memory associate, the discrimi-

---

[12] "This class of thinkers asserts that objects as well as mind and mental activities are all perishing from moment to moment."—From K'uei Chi's commentary on the Chinese version of this *Treatise*.

nated mental representation, appearing as a seemingly former object. Then we speak of this as a memory of what has been already experienced. Therefore, to use a later memory to prove the real existence of a previously seen external object cannot in principle be maintained.

[Question] If, in waking time as well as in a dream, representations may arise although there are no true objects, then, just as the world naturally knows that dream objects are nonexistent, why is it not naturally known of the objects in waking time, since they are the same? Since it is not naturally known that waking objects are nonexistent, how, as in dream consciousness, are the real objects all nothing?

[Answer] This also is no evidence, for the Stanza says:

XVI (*Second part*)

. . . . Before we have awakened we cannot know
That what is seen in the dream does not exist.

Just as in the unawakened state we do not know dream objects are not externally real, but do know it on awaking, even so the world's falsely discriminated recurrent impressions are confused and fevered as in the midst of a dream, all that is seen being wholly unreal; before the true awakening is attained this cannot be naturally known. But if there is a time when we attain that world-transcending knowledge, emancipatory and nondiscriminative, then we call it the true awakening. After this, the purified knowledge of the world which is obtained takes precedence; according to the truth it is clearly understood that those objects are unreal. The principle is the same.

XXXI

TRUE DOCTRINE SHOULD STAND THE TEST

The old Buddhist tale here translated from the Chinese [13] *is taken from a commentary written in 661 A.D. by K'uei Chi, a noted scholar-priest of the T'ang Dynasty, on the philosophical classic represented in the preceding selection. Introduced by K'uei Chi in order to amplify a passing reference to scripture, it reflects none of the subtle metaphysics of its context. Though not original with K'uei Chi, the story is told succinctly and with a dash of genuine Chinese humor.*

Nātaputta the Nigaṇṭha [14] had a disciple named Dīgha Tapassī who one day went to the place where Buddha was staying. Buddha asked Tapassī: "In the doctrine thy master teaches thee which among the three kinds of deeds meriting punishment is reckoned as heaviest?"

He answered saying: "Deeds of the body are heaviest; next, deeds of speech; and last, deeds of thought."

Dīgha Tapassī then asked in return: "What now does Gotama say are the most important deeds?"

Buddha said: "Those of thought are most important. Those of body and speech are lighter."

Dīgha Tapassī then returned home. Nātaputta asked him:

---

[13] Tr. by Clarence H. Hamilton from K'uei Chi's *Wei-shih-er-shih-lun Shu-chi*, which is a commentary on Hsüan Tsang's Chinese version of the philosophical treatise represented in Reading No. XXX. K'uei Chi repeats the story on the authority of the *Chung-a-han Ching* (i.e. the Chinese version of the Madhyamāgama Sūtra). See Bunyiu Nanjio's *Catalogue of the Chinese Translation of the Buddhist Tripiṭaka*, No. 542. A Pāli version of the story of Upāli's conversion may be read in the Majjhima Nikāya, Sutta 56, translated by Lord Chalmers and published in *Further Dialogues of the Buddha*, I, 267-278.

[14] A rival religious teacher, leader of the Jains, by whom he is usually called Mahāvīra. The Jains were a markedly ascetic group, and the Chinese name for Dīgha Tapassī could be humorously translated as "Long on Austerities."

"When you went to his place what did Gotama say?" Dīgha Tapassī told him everything and Nātaputta praised him saying: "Truly thou art my son, born of my word! Well hast thou received my teaching. What thou didst say differs not from it. Thou mayest go in my stead to refute the position of Gotama and bring him here that in the future he may be my disciple."

To this, however, Dīgha Tapassī would not agree. But a wealthy householder, Upāli by name, who humbly served Nātaputta the Nigaṇṭha, was quite ready to go and refute the position taken by Gotama. Dīgha Tapassī told him, This thing ought not to be. In manner and talent for discussion this Gotama immeasurably surpasses other men. Also, he possesses a magic art by which he is able to turn men's hearts, so that countless living beings become his disciples, preferring to go down in defeat before him.

Nātaputta, being incredulous of this, commanded the householder to go. So the householder, having arrived and desiring to refute Buddha's view, forthwith set up his own position, saying: "I maintain that there are three kinds of offense. Those of the body are heaviest; then come those of speech, and last those of thought. Wherefore does Gotama say that mental offenses are heaviest?"

Now at that time the World-honored One was in the Mei-ch'ih-lo country, the city of which required five days just to walk along one side.[15] Buddha asked the householder: "If a man were to commit murder, how many days of killing would it take to finish off the inhabitants of this country?"

The householder answered and said: "In a case of great ability seven days, or perchance ten days or a month."

Again he asked: "If an immortal rishi, becoming enraged, kills by means of a thought, how many days would it take to finish them?"

"In one moment," was the answer, "the people of the country would all be done for."

Still again Buddha asked! "One hundred days, two hundred days, three hundred days spent giving money in charity; or a man entering for one time into the tranquillity of deep meditation—which is superior? Or, here is a man who for a long time has been

[15] In the Pāli version of this story the name of the city is given as Nālandā.

keeping precepts, and there is another who for one time enters the undefiled view—which is superior?"

The householder answered and said: "To enter into meditation and the undefiled view is greatly superior to meritorious acts."

Buddha said: "But how then can the householder say that offenses of body and speech are heavy while those of the mind are very light?"

The householder, being in the wrong, humbly prayed to become a disciple and finally obtained the fruit of realization. Then he of himself made a vow and said: "In the place where I dwell I intend ever to nourish the Three Sacred Treasures [i.e. Buddha, his Law, and his Order]. But as for all Jains, none of them may enter my house."

Having gained the true path, the householder went back to his own home. Nātaputta, wondering why he was so late, sent one to go and search for him. The householder's family folk would not allow him to enter the dwelling. Nātaputta was not able to fathom this and went himself to seek him. The householder in solemn dignity seated himself on the high dais [usually given to honored guests] and had a lower seat placed separately for the reception of Nātaputta. Nātaputta seeing him using the rules in this fashion scolded and reproved the householder.

Then the householder answered and said: "I am not now the man that I was formerly. I now am already superior to thee, being Buddha's disciple. How could it be otherwise?"

But Nātaputta said: "I commanded thee to bring Gotama to be my disciple. Since that may not be, and I now have lost thee again, I shall utter for thy sake a parable." Accordingly he composed the parable and said: "For instance, there is a man who, needing a yü-p'o-lo root [a certain kind of medicinal herb], develops a craving to eat one. He directs a man to enter a pond and search for one in every part of it. The search is unsuccessful, but the man himself pulls up a mandrake. Then, in not obtaining a yü-p'o-lo root, of his own accord he lets fall the mandrake. Thou also art in like case. Not only has the search for Gotama been in vain, but I have instead lost thee. Thou art as the mandrake."

The householder answered and said: "I now make for thee a

parable. There was once a man, by nature very stupid and foolish, who received in marriage a clever wife. After the marriage, in due time being with child, the wife said a son would be born and that a plaything ought to be provided for him. She talked with her husband, who was willing to seek one. When the husband had found a monkey he went back to his wife. The wife said to her husband, You ought to have him washed, dyed and pounded in a mortar; then he will be fit for a plaything. The husband presently hired a man to wash, dye and pound the monkey. That one said to him, It will do to give him a bath, but how can he be dyed and pounded in a mortar? If he were a garment all three things could be done; but the case of a monkey is otherwise! But he bathed it for him; and when the bathing was finished, he put the monkey in hot juice and dyed it. After skin and flesh were already cooked to pieces he pounded them with pestle and mortar. Whereupon all form and semblance were lost; and again it was unfit to be the son's plaything.

"Now thy doctrine is also thus. Since it is not a pure thing, it can only be cleansed. It cannot stand being laid hold of, like the inability [of the monkey] to be dyed. It cannot stand cultivation and practice, like the inability to be pounded in a mortar. How can you command me to receive, maintain, cultivate and study it?"

Nātaputta, thereupon, ashamed and humbled went his way.

PART FOUR
JAPANESE BUDDHIST LITERATURE

XXXII

HŌNEN'S QUEST FOR SALVATION

In Japan no form of Buddhism is more popular than the Pure Land school. Its founder was Hōnen (1133–1212 A.D.). From his original sect (called Jōdo, which is simply the Japanese term for Pure Land), there developed in time several sub-sects, the most notable of which is the Shin Shu (True Sect), established by Hōnen's disciple Shinran (1173–1262). In the following,[1] Hōnen tells how, upon reading a certain Chinese commentary, he became convinced of the great value in repeating the name of Amitabha (Amida in Japanese) in faith. For him this was an experience of arriving at inner certainty and peace.[2]

Hōnen once said, "Having a deep desire to obtain salvation, and with faith in the teachings of the various scriptures, I practice many forms of self-discipline. There are indeed many doctrines in Buddhism, but they may all be summed up in the three learnings—namely, the precepts, meditation, and knowledge, as practiced by the adherents of the Lesser and Greater Vehicles, and the exoteric and esoteric sects. But the fact is that I do not keep even one of the precepts, nor do I attain to any one of the many forms of meditation. A certain priest has said that without the observance of the śila (precepts), there is no such thing as the realization of samādhi. Moreover, the heart of the ordinary unenlightened man, because of his surroundings, is always liable to change, just like

[1] From Shunjō, *Hōnen the Buddhist Saint*, tr. by Harper Havelock Coates and Ryugaku Ishizuka, pp. 185-187.
[2] The Original Vow mentioned in this selection is the vow by which Amitabha determined to create his paradise or Land of Perfect Bliss. The scripture reporting the story of this vow has been translated from Sanskrit by Max Müller as "The Larger Sukhāvatī-Vyūha Sūtra," *Sacred Books of the East*, Vol. 49.

monkeys jumping from one branch to another. It is indeed in a state of confusion, easily moved and with difficulty controlled. In what way does right and indefectible knowledge arise? Without the sword of indefectible knowledge, how can one get free from the chains of evil passion, whence comes evil conduct? And unless one gets free from evil conduct and evil passions, how shall he obtain deliverance from the bondage of birth and death? Alas! What shall I do? What shall I do? The like of us are incompetent to practice the three disciplines of the precepts, meditation, and knowledge.

"And so I inquired of a great many learned men and priests whether there is any other way of salvation than these three disciplines, that is better suited to our poor abilities, but I found none who could either teach me the way or even suggest it to me. At last I went into the library at Kurodani on Mount Hiei, where all the scriptures were, all by myself, and, with a heavy heart, read them all through. While doing so, I hit upon a passage in Zendō's *Commentary on the Meditation Sūtra,* which runs as follows: "Whether walking or standing, sitting or lying, only repeat the name of Amida with all your heart. Never cease the practice of it even for a moment. This is the very work which unfailingly issues in salvation, for it is in accordance with the Original Vow of that Buddha." On reading this I was impressed with the fact that even ignorant people like myself, by reverent meditation upon this passage and an entire dependence upon the truth in it, never forgetting the repetition of Amida's sacred name, may lay the foundation for that good Karma which will with absolute certainty eventuate in birth into the Blissful Land. And not only was I led to believe in this teaching bequeathed by Zendō, but also earnestly to follow the great Vow of Amida. And especially was that passage deeply inwrought into my very soul which says, "For it is in accordance with the Original Vow of that Buddha."

XXXIII

SHINRAN'S CONFESSION

Like Hōnen before him, Shinran taught reliance on the merits of Amida (Amitabha), the Buddha of Infinite Light. He put less stress, however, on the mere invocation of his name. For Shinran, faith is the essential thing, not works in any category. No matter how great the sinner, if he has faith in Amida he will be born into the Pure Land after death. In the following verses [3] he freely confesses his sense of personal unworthiness, but affirms his trust in "the divine promise of Infinite Wisdom."

> Though I seek my refuge in the true faith of the Pure Land,
> > Yet hath not mine heart been truly sincere.
> > Deceit and untruth are in my flesh,
> > And in my soul is no clear shining.
>
> In their outward seeming are all men diligent and truth speaking,
> > But in their souls are greed and anger and unjust deceitfulness,
> > And in their flesh do lying and cunning triumph.
>
> Too strong for me is the evil of my heart. I cannot overcome it.
> > Therefore is my soul like unto the poison of serpents;
> > Even my righteous deeds, being mingled with this poison,
> > Must be named the deeds of deceitfulness.
>
> Shameless though I be and having no truth in my soul,
> > Yet the virtue of the Holy Name, the gift of Him that is enlightened,
> > Is spread throughout the world through my words, although I am as I am.

[3] Tr. from the Japanese by S. Yamabe and L. Adams Beck, in *Buddhist Psalms*. "Wisdom of the East Series," pp. 86-87.

There is no mercy in my soul. The good of my fellow man
  is not dear in mine eyes.
If it were not for the Ark of Mercy,
The divine promise of the Infinite Wisdom,
How should I cross the Ocean of Misery?

I, whose mind is filled with cunning and deceit as the
  poison of reptiles,
Am impotent to practice righteous deeds.
If I sought not refuge in the gift of our Father,
I should die the death of the shameless.

XXXIV

HAKUIN'S SONG OF MEDITATION

Meditation as a method of religious discipline has been present in Buddhism from the beginning. In the Far East, however, a distinct meditative sect has grown up about the practice with characteristics of its own. In China it is known as Ch'an, in Japan as Zen, both terms meaning Meditation. Philosophically, the Zen Sect favors the Doctrine of Emptiness as found in the "Essence of the Wisdom Sūtra," which is daily chanted in the monasteries. Its basic aim, nevertheless, is not philosophical but mystical. It seeks to cultivate a special sudden awakening to a new viewpoint on things, an inner spiritual experience which is not further explicable because it is not an intellectual realization. Meditation is for the purpose of bringing on this experience, but is not to be identified with the awakening itself. In the poem here given,[4] the high value of meditation is extolled by Hakuin (1685–1768 A.D.), the founder of modern Japanese Zen.

[4] From Daisetz Teitaro Suzuki, *Manual of Zen Buddhism*, pp. 183-184.

Sentient beings are primarily all the Buddhas:
It is like ice and water:
Apart from water no ice can exist;
Outside sentient beings, where do we find the
   Buddhas?
Not knowing how near the Truth is,
People seek it far away—what a pity!
They are like him who, in the midst of water,
Cries in thirst so imploringly;
They are like the son of a rich man
Who wandered away among the poor.
The reason why we transmigrate through the six
   worlds,
Is because we are lost in the darkness of ignorance;
Going astray further and further in the darkness,
When are we able to get away from birth-and-
   death?

As regards the Meditation practiced in the Mahā-
   yāna,
We have no words to praise it fully:
The virtues of perfection such as charity, morality,
   etc.,
And the invocation of the Buddha's name, confes-
   sion, and ascetic discipline,
And many other good deeds of merit—
All these issue from the practice of Meditation.
Even those who have practiced it just for one
   sitting,
Will see all their evil karma wiped clean;
Nowhere will they find the evil paths,
But the Pure Land will be near at hand.
With a reverential heart, let them to this Truth
Listen even for once,
And let them praise it, and gladly embrace it,
And they will surely be blessed most infinitely.

For such as, reflecting within themselves,
Testify to the truth of self-nature,
To the truth that self-nature is no-nature,
They have really gone beyond the ken of sophistry.
For them opens the gate of the oneness of cause and effect,
And straight runs the path of non-duality and non-trinity.
Abiding with the not-particular which is in particulars,
Whether going or returning, they remain forever unmoved;
Taking hold of the not-thought which lies in thoughts,
In every act of theirs they hear the voice of the Truth.
How boundless the sky of Samādhi unfettered!
How transparent the perfect moonlight of the Fourfold Wisdom!
At that moment what do they lack?
As the Truth eternally calm reveals itself to them,
This very earth is the Lotus Land of Purity,
And this body is the body of the Buddha.

XXXV

NICHIREN'S VOW

In the history of Japanese Buddhism there is no more colorful personality than Nichiren (1222-1282), founder of the sect which bears his name. Born son of a fisherman, he entered a monastery in boyhood, and became an ordained monk at the age of fifteen. Early in his career he became convinced that the perfect truth of Buddhism is fully expressed in the Lotus Scripture alone. He also decided that amid the decadence of the times in which he lived this truth was obscured and lost through false teachings and practices of current Buddhist sects. Ardent in his devotion to the Lotus of Truth, he became vehement in criticism and denunciation of other forms of Buddhist belief. He also proved fearless in pointing out the degeneracy of the people and the foolishness of their rulers. This brought on persecution and opposition. Twice he was sent into exile by the government. Yet followers multiplied. These he organized into the Nichiren Sect and taught to chant the sacred name of the Lotus Scripture. The salvation of Japan itself, he believed, depended upon return to the truth of this scripture, and he pointed to the threatened invasion by the Mongols as evidence. To a degree Nichiren combined qualities of saint, crusader, prophet and nationalist in his make-up. In the following selection we have a characteristic utterance.[5]

> Finally, let the celestial beings withdraw their protection, let all perils come upon me, even so will I dedicate my life to this cause. . . . Be it in weal, be it in woe, to desert the Lotus of Truth means to fall to the hells. I will be firm in my Great Vow. Let me face all manner of threats and temptations. Should one say to me, "Thou mightest ascend the throne of Japan if thou wouldst abandon the Scripture and expect future bliss through belief in the meditation on Amida; or thy parents shall suffer capital punishment unless thou utterest the name of the Buddha Amida," etc.—such temptation I shall meet unshaken, and shall never be allured by them, unless my principles shall be shattered by a sage's refutation of them. Any other perils shall be the dust before a storm. I will be the Pillar of Japan; I will be the Eyes of Japan; I will be the Great Vessel of Japan. Inviolable shall remain these oaths.

[5] Tr. by Masaharu Anesaki, in his *Nichiren, the Buddhist Prophet*, p. 73.

XXXVI

THE IDEAL BUDDHIST LAYMAN

One of the Sūtras most greatly esteemed in Japan is devoted to portraying the character and teachings of a lay Buddhist by the name of Vimalakīrti. Composed originally in Sanskrit, it was translated into Chinese by Kumārajīva some time between 401–413 A.D. Later, in Japan, Prince Regent Shōtoku Taishi (573–621 A.D.), who promoted the introduction of Buddhism into his country, wrote a commentary on this scripture. The purpose of the Sūtra is to show that it is possible to live the life of a saintly aspirant to Buddhahood while living in the midst of the world— to be in the world but not of it. Vimalakīrti is represented as wiser and better than all the monastic teachers with whom he has discourse. In the following selection his virtues are set forth.[6]

At that time, there dwelt in the great city of Vaiśāli a wealthy householder named Vimalakīrti. Having done homage to the countless Buddhas of the past, doing many good works, attaining to acquiescence in the Eternal Law, he was a man of wonderful eloquence,

Exercising supernatural powers, obtaining all the Dhāranīs, arriving at the state of fearlessness,

Repressing all evil enmities, reaching the gate of profound truth, walking in the way of wisdom,

Acquainted with the necessary means, fulfilling the Great Vows, comprehending the past and the future of the intentions of all beings, understanding also both their strength and weakness of mind,

Ever pure and excellent in the way of the Buddha, remaining loyal to the Mahāyāna,

[6] From Vimalakīrti-nirdeśa Sūtra, Ch. 2. English translation by Hokei Idumi, in *The Eastern Buddhist*, Vol. III, No. 2 (July-August-September, 1924), pp. 138-141. The passage has been slightly edited and condensed in the above presentation.

Deliberating before action, following the conduct of Buddha, great in mind as the ocean,

Praised by all the Buddhas, revered by all the disciples and all the gods such as a Śakra and Brahman king, the lord of this world,

Residing in Vaiśāli only for the sake of the necessary means for saving creatures, abundantly rich, ever careful of the poor, pure in self-discipline, obedient to all precepts,

Removing all anger by the practice of patience, removing all sloth by the practice of diligence, removing all distraction of mind by intent meditation, removing all ignorance by fullness of wisdom;

Though he is but a simple layman, yet observing the pure monastic discipline;

Though living at home, yet never desirous of anything;

Though possessing a wife and children, always exercising pure virtues;

Though surrounded by his family, holding aloof from worldly pleasures;

Though using the jeweled ornaments of the world, yet adorned with spiritual splendor;

Though eating and drinking, yet enjoying the flavor of the rapture of meditation;

Though frequenting the gambling house, yet leading the gamblers into the right path;

Though coming in contact with heresy, yet never letting his true faith be impaired;

Though having a profound knowledge of worldly learning, yet ever finding pleasure in things of the spirit as taught by Buddha;

Revered by all as the first among those who were worthy of reverence;

Governing both the old and young as a righteous judge;

Though profiting by all the professions, yet far above being absorbed by them;

Benefiting all beings, going wheresoever he pleases, protecting all beings as a judge with righteousness;

Leading all with the Doctrine of the Mahāyāna when in the seat of discussion;

Ever teaching the young and ignorant when entering the hall of learning;

Manifesting to all the error of passion when in the house of debauchery; persuading all to seek the higher things when at the shop of the wine dealer;

Preaching the Law when among wealthy people as the most honorable of their kind;

Dissuading the rich householders from covetousness when among them as the most honorable of their kind;

Teaching kshatriyas [i.e. warriors] patience when among them ... etc.

Removing arrogance when among brāhmans. . . .

Teaching justice to the great ministers. . . .

Teaching loyalty and filial piety to the princes. . . .

Teaching honesty to the ladies of the court when among them ... etc.

Persuading the masses to cherish the virtue of merits. . . .

Instructing in highest wisdom the Brahman gods. . . .

Showing the transient nature of the world to the Śakra gods. . . .

Protecting all beings when among the guardians as the most honorable of their kind;

—Thus by such countless means Vimalakīrti, the wealthy householder, rendered benefit to all beings.

XXXVII

PHILOSOPHY OF DIALECTICAL CRITICISM

In the second century A.D., a notable Indian Buddhist thinker, Nāgārjuna by name, undertook to emphasize the importance of intuitional enlightenment by showing the absurdity of all intellectual determinations and the logical impossibility of all sensible and mental experience. Every alternative of thought, even every doctrinal concept of earlier Buddhist teachers, was demonstrated as too contradictory for valid apprehension of final truth. Thus he carried to its explicit logical extreme the doctrine of "The Void" (Śūnya), already brought before us in Selections XXV and XXVI. In all this, Nāgārjuna's purpose was to point beyond the limits of phenomenal existence by demonstrating its relative, logically contradictory character. The aphorisms of his Mādhyamika Śāstra (400 in all) became basic to Mahāyāna Buddhism and are known among intellectuals of all its schools in Japan, China, Mongolia and Tibet. The following verses from the first and twenty-fifth chapters of that work [7] contain his critique of the concepts of Causality and Nirvāṇa. They exemplify the method he applies to all existential determinations. It is intended to clear the mind of all illusions obstructing insight into final (inexpressible) reality.

EXAMINATION OF CAUSALITY

I

There absolutely are no things,
Nowhere and none, that arise [anew],
Neither out of themselves, nor out of non-self,
Nor out of both, nor at random.

II

Four can be the conditions
[Of every thing produced],
Its cause, its object, its foregoing moment,
Its most decisive factor.

III

In these conditions we can find
No self-existence of the entities.
Where self-existence is deficient,
Relational existence also lacks.

---

[7] From Nāgārjuna's Mādhyamika Śāstra. Tr. by T. I. Stcherbatsky, in his *The Conception of Buddhist Nirvāṇa*, pp. 71-78.

IV

No energies in causes,
Nor energies outside them.
No causes without energies,
Nor causes that possess them.

V

Let those facts be causes
With whom coordinated other facts arise
Non-causes will they be,
So far the other facts have not arisen.

VI

Neither non-Ens nor Ens
Can have a cause.
If non-Ens, whose the cause?
If Ens, whatfore the cause?

VII

Neither an Ens nor a non-Ens,
Nor any Ens-non-Ens,
No element is really turned out.
How can we then assume
The possibility of a producing cause?

VIII

A mental Ens is reckoned as an element,
Separately from its objective [counterpart].
Now, if it [begins] by having no objective counterpart,
How can it get one afterward?

IX

If [separate] elements do not exist,
Nor is it possible for them to disappear.
The moment which immediately precedes
Is thus impossible. And if 'tis gone,
How can it be a cause?

X

If entities are relative,
They have no real existence.
The [formula] "this being, that appears"
Then loses every meaning.

XI

Neither in any of the single causes
Nor in all of them together
Does the [supposed] result reside.
How can you out of them extract
What in them never did exist?

XII

Supposing from these causes does appear
What never did exist in them,
Out of non-causes then
Why does it not appear?

XIII

The result is cause-possessor,
But causes are not even self-possessors.
How can result be cause-possessor,
If of nonself-possessors it be a result?

XIV

There is, therefore, no cause-possessor,
Nor is there an effect without a cause.
If altogether no effect arises,
[How can we then distinguish]
Between the causes and non-causes?

EXAMINATION OF NIRVĀNA

I

If every thing is relative,
No [real] origination, no [real] annihilation,
How is Nirvāṇa then conceived?
Through what deliverance, through what annihilation?

II

Should every thing be real in substance,
No [new] creation, no [new] destruction,
How would Nirvāṇa then be reached?
Through what deliverance, through what annihilation?

III

What neither is released, nor is it ever reached,
What neither is annihilation, nor is it eternality,
What never disappears, nor has it been created,
This is Nirvāṇa. It escapes precision.

IV

Nirvāṇa, first of all, is not a kind of Ens,
It would then have decay and death.
There altogether is no Ens
Which is not subject to decay and death.

V

If Nirvāṇa is Ens,
It is produced by causes—
Nowhere and none the entity exists
Which would not be produced by causes.

VI

If Nirvāṇa is Ens,
How can it lack substratum;
There whatsoever is no Ens
Without any substratum.

VII

If Nirvāṇa is not an Ens,
Will it be then a non-Ens?
Wherever there is found no Ens,
There neither is a [corresponding] non-Ens.

VIII

Now, if Nirvāṇa is a non-Ens,
How can it then be independent?
For sure, an independent non-Ens
Is nowhere to be found.

IX

Coordinated here or caused are [separate things]:
We call this world Phenomenal;
But just the same is called Nirvāṇa,
When from Causality abstracted.

X

The Buddha has declared
That Ens and non-Ens should be both rejected.
Neither as Ens nor as a non-Ens
Nirvāṇa therefore is conceived.

XI

If Nirvāṇa were both Ens and non-Ens,
Final Deliverance would be also both,
Reality and unreality together.
This never could be possible!

XII

If Nirvāṇa were both Ens and non-Ens,
Nirvāṇa could not be uncaused.
Indeed the Ens and the non-Ens
Are both dependent on causation.

XIII

How can Nirvāṇa represent
An Ens and a non-Ens together?
Nirvāṇa is indeed uncaused,
Both Ens and non-Ens are productions.

XIV

How can Nirvāṇa represent
[The place] of Ens and of non-Ens together,
As light and darkness [in one spot]
They cannot simultaneously be present.

XV

If it were clear, indeed,
What an Ens means, and what a non-Ens,
We could then understand the doctrine
About Nirvāṇa being neither Ens nor non-Ens

XVI

If Nirvāṇa is neither Ens nor non-Ens,
No one can really understand
This doctrine which proclaims at once
Negation of them both together.

XVII

What is the Buddha after his Nirvāṇa?
Does he exist or does he not exist,
Or both, or neither?
We never will conceive it!

XVIII

What is the Buddha then at lifetime?
Does he exist, or does he not exist,
Or both, or neither?
We never will conceive it!

XIX

There is no difference at all
Between Nirvāṇa and Saṃsāra.
There is no difference at all
Between Saṃsāra and Nirvāṇa.

XX

What makes the limit of Nirvāṇa
Is also then the limit of Saṃsāra.
Between the two we cannot find
The slightest shade of difference.

XXI

[Insoluble are antinomic] views
Regarding what exists beyond Nirvāṇa,
Regarding what the end of this world is,
Regarding its beginning.

XXII

Since everything is relative [we do not know],
What is finite and what is infinite,
What means finite and infinite at once,
What means negation of both issues?

XXIII

What is identity, and what is difference?
What is eternity, what noneternity,
What means eternity and noneternity together,
What means negation of both issues?

XXIV

The bliss consists in the cessation of all thought,
In the quiescence of Plurality.
No [separate] Reality was preached at all,
Nowhere and none by Buddha!

PART FIVE
TIBETAN BUDDHIST LITERATURE

XXXVIII

THE STORY OF THE BODISAT VISVANTARA

One class of Buddhist literature is known as Jātaka or "Birth Stories." These are legends, edifying or entertaining as the case may be, concerning events in previous existences of Buddha. In these he appears as a bodhisattva, i.e. a future Buddha or Buddha-to-be, one who through self-sacrificing, compassionate deeds in many successive lives is on the way to become a Buddha. In Tibet, the favorite story of this kind is that of Prince Viśvantara, which is either recited or acted as a drama. Tradition has it that Viśvantara was the last incarnation of Buddha before his rebirth as Gotama. He is represented as carrying out the Buddhist virtue of selfless generosity to the uttermost. While the legend is found in the literature of Southern Buddhism also, the Tibetan version is the more poetic and pathetic. To Western minds its exaggeration is extravagant, but hyperbole is an Eastern way of emphasizing an idea.[1]

VIŚVANTARA

In long past times King Viśvāmitra reigned in the city of Viśvanāgara. As a king of the law, according to the law he ruled over that city, which was blessed with wealth, plenty, prosperity, fruitfulness, and a large population, richly provided with rice, sugar cane, oxen, and buffaloes, and free from disease, discord, quarrels, uproar, strife, and robbery. The king's faith was pure and his mind virtuous; he bethought himself of his own welfare and that of others; he was full of compassion, constant in magnanimity, and kindly toward mankind.

It came to pass that his wife conceived, and, after a space of

---

[1] In Schiefner and Ralston, *Tibetan Tales, Derived from Indian Sources*, pp. 257-272. Tr. from the Tibetan of the Kahgyur by F. Anton von Schiefner, and from Schiefner's German version into English by W. R. S. Ralston.

eight or nine months, gave birth to a fine, well-formed, handsome boy, whose complexion was the color of gold, his head canopy-like, his arms long, his forehead high-arched, his eyebrows interlacing, his nose aquiline, all his limbs and joints complete. When his birthday feast was celebrated after his birth, his kinsmen proceeded to give him a name. They said, "As the boy is King Viśvāmitra's son he shall be called Viśvantara." To the boy Viśvantara were given eight nurses, two for carrying, two for suckling, two for cleansing, and two for playing, who fed him on milk, curdled milk, butter, melted butter, butter-foam, and divers other excellent kinds of nutriment, so that he grew rapidly like a lotus in a pool. When he had grown up and learned writing, counting, and hand-reckoning, he applied himself to all the arts and accomplishments which befit one of the Kshatriya class who has been consecrated to be a king, a ruler provided with riches, might, and heroism, a subduer of the whole orb. Such are riding on elephants and horses, driving in a car, handling of a sword and bow, advancing and retreating, flinging an iron hook, slinging, shooting missiles, striking, cutting, stabbing, seizing, marching, and the five methods of shooting. The young Viśvantara, in whom dwelt pure faith and virtuous feelings, was considerate as to his own welfare and that of others, compassionate and addicted to magnanimity, kindly toward men, of a yielding and generous nature, bestowing presents freely and quite dispassionately, and assiduous in giving away. When men heard of this excessive generosity on his part, numberless crowds came to beg of him, whom he sent away with their expectations completely fulfilled.

One day the Bodisat Viśvantara drove out of the excellent city to the park, in a splendid chariot, gleaming with jewels, gold, silver, steel, coral, lapis-lazuli, turquoises, rubies, and sapphires; constructed of sandalwood; covered with skins of lions, tigers, and bears, its four horses rushing along with the swiftness of the wind, resonant with bells of gold and silver. Some brāhmans versed in the Vedas met him and said, "O Kshatriya youth, may you be victorious!" And they added thereto, "Through the whole world are you renowned as one who gives all things away. Therefore it is meet that you should confer this chariot as a gift on the brāhmans." When they had thus spoken, the Bodisat Viśvantara swiftly alighted from the chariot, and, while with joyful heart he gave the chariot to the brāhmans, he said, "As I have given away the chariot with the greatest pleasure, so may I, giving away the Three Worlds, become possessed of the greatest insight!"

Another time he was riding on the elephant Rājyavardhana, which in whiteness equaled jasmine blossoms, white lotuses, snow, silver, and the clouds, which was of a remarkable size and provided with well-formed feet and trunk, and which strode along like the elephant Airāvaṇa, marked with the signs of distinguished gifts, and remarkable for its capacity. On it, followed by the troop of very devoted slaves, friends, and servants, like unto the moon surrounded by the starry host, he rode, as the spring was come, to the forest park, wherein the trees and the flowers were blooming, and the flamingoes, cranes, peacocks, parrots, mainas, cuckoos, and pheasants were calling. There came up hastily unto Prince Viśvantara, certain brāhmans who were engaged in discussion, and said to him: "Kshatriya prince, may you be victorious!" And they added thereto, "In the world with beings divine and not divine you are renowned as an all-giver. Therefore it is meet that you should give us this splendid elephant." When they had said this, the Bodisat swiftly alighted from the splendid elephant, and having presented that most splendid elephant to them with the utmost good humor, he said, "As I have given the elephant to the brāhmans with the greatest pleasure, so may I, after I have given away the Three Worlds, become possessed of perfect insight!"

When it became known that King Viśvāmitra's son, Visvantara, had given the splendid elephant Rājyavardhana to the brāhmans who were engaged in discussion, and King Viśvāmitra heard the news, he became angry, and he sent for Prince Viśvantara and ordered him to quit the country. Discarded by his father, Viśvantara reflected that he, striving after completest insight, clothed with the armor of virtue out of good will toward the whole world, had given away even his elephant; that so long as he dwelt at home he had bestowed gifts according to his means; that dwelling in the penance forest he had to strive intensely; that as he was not capable of refusing requests, he would rather quit his home and go into the penance forest. Thereupon the Bodisat, after having pronounced a strong vow, went to his wife, Madrī, and told her everything. As soon as she had heard his words she joined the palms of her hands, and, with heart fearful of being parted from the loved one, she said to the Bodisat, "O lord, if this be so, I too will go into the penance forest. Parted from you, O lord, I am not capable of living a single instant longer. And why? As the sky when it is deprived of the moon, as the earth when it is deprived of water, so is the wife who is deprived of her husband."

The Bodisat said, "There is no doubt that we must ultimately be parted, for such is the way of the world. You are accustomed to excellent food and drink, clothes and couches, and therefore you are of a very delicate constitution. In the penance forest it is necessary to sleep on grass and leaves, to feed on roots, flowers, and fruits, and to walk on a ground which is covered with millet and thorns and splinters, to keep constantly to one kind of food, to practice magnanimity toward all beings, and to offer hospitality to those who appear unexpectedly. As even there I shall undoubtedly bestow gifts according to my means, you must feel absolutely no regret on that account. Therefore you ought to think this over well for a time."

Madrī replied, "O lord, so long as I am able, I will follow after you." The Bodisat said, "If this be so, be mindful of your vow."

Then the Bodisat went to his father, paid him reverence with his head, and said, "O father, be pleased to forgive me my fault, the giving away of the elephant. As I am now going forth from the city into the forest, your treasury, O king, will not become empty." The king, losing his breath from grief at the parting, said with tremulous voice, "O son, give up making presents and remain here." The Bodisat replied, "The earth and its mountains may perhaps be destined to overthrow; but I, O lord of the earth, cannot turn aside my mind from giving."

After saying these words he went away, mounted a chariot along with his son, daughter, and wife, and went forth from the good city, hundreds of thousands of the townspeople and country folks attending him with lamentation. A certain man who heard this wailing and lament, and saw such great crowds streaming toward the city gate, asked another man, "Hey, friend, wherefore has so great a multitude set up such a lamentation?" "Honored sir," was the reply, "do not you know in what way the king's own son has been sent away from here, because he persistently took pleasure in giving?"

When the prince, together with his wife and children, had reached the margin of the forest, all the people who formed his retinue raised a loud cry of lament. But so soon as it was heard, the Bodisat addressed the retinue which had come forth from the good city, and ordered it to turn back, saying—

"However long anything may be loved and held dear, yet separation from it is undoubtedly imminent. Friends and relatives must undoubtedly be severed from what is dearest to them, as from the trees of the hermitage wherein they have rested from the fatigues of the journey. Therefore, when ye reflect that all over the world men are powerless against separation from their friends, ye must for the sake of peace strengthen your unsteady minds by unfailing exertion."

When the Bodisat had journeyed three hundred yojanas, a brāhman came to him and said, "O Kshatriya prince, I have come three hundred yojanas because I have heard of your virtue. It is meet that you should give me the splendid chariot as a recompense for my fatigue."

Madrī could not bear this, and she addressed the brāhman in angry speech. "Alas! this brāhman, who even in the forest entreats the king's son for a gift, has a merciless heart. Does no pity arise within him when he sees the prince fallen from his royal splendor?"

The Bodisat said, "Find no fault with the brāhman."

"Why not?"

"Madrī, if there were no people of that kind who long after riches there would also be no giving, and in that case how could we, inhabitants of the earth, become possessed of insight? As giving and the other Pāramitās [or virtues essential to a Buddhaship] rightly comprise the highest virtue, the Bodisats constantly attain to the highest insight."

Thereupon the Bodisat bestowed the chariot and horses on that brāhman with exceeding great joy, and said, "O brāhman, by means of this gift of the chariot, a present free from the blemish of grudging, may I be enabled to direct the car of the sinless law directed by the most excellent Rishi!" When Viśvantara had with exceeding great joy bestowed on the brāhman the splendid chariot, he took Prince Krishna on his shoulder, and Madrī took Princess Jālinī. They went forth into the forest, and at length arrived at the forest of penance.

In that penance-forest Viśvantara dwelt, after he had taken the vow which pleased his heart. One day, when Madrī had gone to collect roots and fruits in the penance-forest, a brāhman came to Viśvantara, and said, "O prince of Kshatriya race, may you be victorious! As I have no slave, and wander about alone with my staff, therefore is it meet that you should give me your two children." As the Bodisat Viśvantara, after hearing these words, hesitated a little about giving his beloved children, the brāhman said to the Bodisat—

"O prince of Kshatriya race, as I have heard that you are the giver of all things, therefore do I ask why you still ponder over this request of mine. You are renowned all over the earth as the possessor of a compassion which gives away all things: you are bound to act constantly in conformity with this renown."

After hearing these words the Bodisat said to the brāhman, "O great brāhman, if I had to give away my own life I should not hesitate for a single moment. How, then, should I think differently if I had to give away my children? O great brāhman, under these circumstances I have bethought me as to how the children, when given by me, if I do give away these two children who have grown up in the forest, will live full of sorrow on account of their separation from their mother. And inasmuch as many will blame me, in that with excessive mercilessness I have given away the children and not myself, therefore is it better that you, O brāhman, should take me."

Then said the brāhman to Viśvantara, "O prince of Kshatriya race, descended from a great kingly family, as I have perceived how all over this earth your virtue is extolled, your goodness which takes pity on all beings—the presents, the hospitality, and the honor with which you welcome śramanas, brāhmans, and strangers, and fulfill all the expectations of the poor and needy, the helpless and the hungry—it is not right that I, after having come to you, should remain without a present and deprived of the fruit of my journey, and that, with the knowledge that I have not obtained it, all the hopes which my mind had cherished should be brought to nought. Therefore is it meet that you, fulfilling my hopes, should give me the children. And why? One who gave away the earth, clothed with the ocean as with a garment, possessing the cornfields as its incomparable eyes, the mighty hills as the upper parts of its body with breasts, and supporting towns and villages, would not be equal in might to you."

When the Bodisat Viśvantara had heard these words of the brāhman, he laid aside the longing which clung to the children, saying to himself, "If I give the two children to the brāhman, Madrī and I will feel the pain of parting with the children. But if I do not give them to him, then I shall prove faithless to my vow, and the brāhman, disappointed in his hopes, will go away as he came. If he receives them, despairing grief for the loss of my children will be my lot upon earth. If I act otherwise, I break my promise and my vow disappears."

Then the Bodisat Viśvantara determined to give up his beloved children, and he said, "Well, then, this takes place in order that, by means of a hundred kinds of penance, I, like a pillared transit bridge resembling the full moon with spotless visage, may save from the sea of troubles, containing manifold terrors, those who sink into its bottomless depths." After he had uttered these words with an untroubled countenance, his eyes filled with tears, and he gave his two children to the brāhman, and said, "As I am to obtain a very great recompense in return for the gift of the children, I shall save the world from the ocean of revolution."

Immediately after the surrender of the children, the earth quaked in a sixfold manner. When the ascetics who dwelt in the forest, terrified by the earthquake, asked one another by whose power the earth had been shaken in so intolerable a manner, and wished to know who it was who possessed such power, an old ascetic of the Vaśishtha race, who was versed in the meanings of signs, made the matter known to them, saying, "The earth has doubtless been set in movement because Viśvantara, in order that he may completely redeem men reduced to despair by trouble, has given up his two bright-eyed, beloved children, who dwelt in the penance-forest, partaking of fruit and water."

Now, when the two children saw that their father was about to give them away, they touched Viśvantara's feet, uttering mournful cries, and joining the palms of their hands, and saying, "O father, will you give us away in the absence of our mother? Be content to give us up after we have seen her." Then the Bodisat gave way under the grief which had laid hold of his mind, and his face was wet with tears as he embraced his two children and said, "O children, in my heart there is no unkindness, but only merciful compassion. As I have manifested virtue for the salvation of the whole world, I give you away, whereby I may attain unto complete insight, and, having myself obtained rest, may save the worlds which lie, deprived of support, in the ocean of woes."

When the children perceived that their father's resolve was firm to give them up, they paid honor to his feet with their heads, laid their palms together, and said with soft complaint, "If you have severed the cord, we have this to say: grant us forbearance. O father, be pleased to utter the words. Every fault which we, as children, have committed against you, our superior, or any words at any time uttered by us, which displeased you, or anything in which, not obeying you, we have wrongly left aught undone—grant us forgiveness of these things, regarding them as the faults of children."

After they had thus spoken, and had paid reverence to their father, and three times encompassed him, they went forth from the hermitage, ever looking back with tearful eyes, keeping in their hearts those things which they had to say to their superior. The Bodisat consoled them with compassionate words, and then, desiring to attain to the highest insight, he betook himself to a hut made of leaves in the forest of penance.

Scarcely had the children gone away, when the system of the three thousand worlds quaked six times. Many thousands of gods filled the air with sounds of shouting and rejoicing, and cried, "Oh the great deed of surrender! Truly is he worthy of being wondered at, whose mind remains constant even after the surrender of both his children."

Meanwhile Madrī had set off for the hermitage, carrying roots and fruits, and when the earth shook, she hurried on all the faster toward the hermitage. A certain deity, who perceived that she might hinder the surrender which the Bodisat proposed to make for the salvation of the world, assumed the form of a lioness and barred her way. Then Madrī said to this wife of the King of the Beasts, "O wife of the King of the Beasts, full of wantonness, wherefore do you bar my way? In order that I may remain truly irreproachablė, make way for me that I may pass swiftly on. Moreover, you are the wife of the King of the Beasts, and I am the spouse of the Lion of Princes, so that we are of similar rank. Therefore, O Queen of the Beasts, leave the road clear for me."

When Madrī had thus spoken, the deity, who had assumed the form of the lioness, turned aside from the way. Madrī reflected for a moment, recognizing inauspicious omens, for the air resounded with wailing notes and the beings inhabiting the forest gave forth sorrowful sounds, and she came to the conclusion that some disaster had certainly taken place in the hermitage, and said, "As my eye twitches, as the birds utter cries, as fear comes upon me, both my children have certainly been given away; as the earth quakes, as my heart trembles, as my body grows weak, my two children have certainly been given away."

With a hundred thousand similar thoughts of woe she hastened toward the hermitage. Entering therein she looked mournfully around, and, not seeing the children, she sadly, with trembling heart, followed the traces left on the ground of the hermitage. "Here the boy Kṛishṇa and his sister were wont to play with the young gazelles; here is the house which they twain made out of earth; these are the playthings of the two children. As they are not to be seen, it is possible that they may have gone unseen by me into the hut of foliage and may be sleeping there." Thus thinking and hoping to see the children, she laid aside the roots and fruits, and with tearful eyes embraced her husband's feet, asking, "O lord, whither have the boy and girl gone?" Viśvaṇtara replied, "A brāhman came to me full of hope. To him have I given the two children. Thereat rejoice." When he had spoken these words, Madrī fell to the ground like a gazelle pierced by a poisoned arrow, and struggled like a fish taken out of the water. Like a crane robbed of her young ones she uttered sad cries. Like a cow whose calf has died, she gave forth many a sound of wailing. Then she said, "Shaped like young lotuses, with hands whose flesh is as tender as a young lotus leaf, my two children are suffering, are undergoing pain, wherever they have gone. Slender as young gazelles, gazelle-eyed, delighting in the lairs of the gazelles, what sufferings are my children now undergoing in the power of strangers? With tearful eyes and sad sobbing, enduring cruel sufferings, now that they are no longer seen by me, they live downtrodden among needy men. They who were nourished at my breast, who used to eat roots, flowers, and fruits, they who, experiencing indulgence, were ever wont to enjoy themselves to the full, those two children of mine now undergo great sufferings. Severed from their mother and their family, deserted by the cruelty of their relatives, thrown together with sinful men, my two children are now undergoing great suffering. Constantly tormented by hunger and thirst, made slaves by those into whose power they have fallen, they will doubtless experience the pangs of despair. Surely I have committed some terrible sin in a previous existence, in severing hundreds of beings from their dearest ones. Therefore do I now lament like a cow which has lost its calf. If there exists any exorcism by which I can gain over all beings, so shall my two children, after having been made slaves, be by it rendered free."

Then Madrī, looking upon the thick-foliaged trees which the children had planted and tended, embraced them tenderly, and said, "The children fetched water in small pitchers, and dropped water on the leaves. You, O trees, did the children suckle, as though ye had been possessed of souls." Further on, when she saw the young gazelles with which the children used to play, standing in the hermitage, she sadly said, gently wailing, "With the desire of seeing their playfellows do the young gazelles visit the spot, searching among the plants, offering companionship with my never-ending woe." Afterwards, when the footprints on the road along which the children had gone became interrupted, and she saw that their footprints did not lie in a straight line, but in all sorts of directions, she was seized by bitter anguish and cried, "As the footprints point to dragging along and some of them to swiftness of pace, you must surely have driven them on with blows, O most merciless brāhman. How have my children fared with tender feet, their throats breathing with difficulty, their voices reduced to weakness, their pretty lower lips trembling, like gazelles timidly looking around?"

Observing how she bore herself and uttered complaints, the Bodisat exerted himself to exhort his wife with a series of such and such words about instability, and said, "Not for the sake of renown, nor out of anger, have I given away your two children; for the salvation of all beings have I given the children, whom it was hard to give. By giving up the objects which it is hardest to give up—children and wife—may one, like the great souls, attain to the completest insight. O Madrī, as I cling closely to giving, I have given for the redemption of the world the children whom it was hard to give. My purpose is to sacrifice all things, to give myself, my wife, my children, and my treasures."

When after a time Madrī had recovered her strength of mind, she said to the Bodisat: "I will in nothing be a hindrance to you. Let your mind be constant. If you wish to give me, too, give me without hesitation. As soon as, O courageous one, you have attained to that, for the sake of which you give up that which is connected with difficulty, save all beings from revolution."

When the king of the gods, Śakra, perceived this marvelous endurance on the part of the Bodisat, and the striving of Madrī, and their deeds very hard to be accomplished, he descended from heaven, surrounded by the company of the thirty-three gods, into the hermitage, and lighted it up with great brilliance. Remaining in the air, he said to the Bodisat: "Inasmuch as after this fashion, O mighty one, in the foolish world, the mind of which is bound fast by knots of ignorance, in the world which is fettered by the bonds of a mind which pays homage to enjoyment, you alone, superior to passion, have given up the children in whom you delighted, you have certainly attained to this degree through stainless and joyless tranquillity."

After gratifying the Bodisat with these words, the king of the gods, Śakra, said to himself: As this man, when alone and without support, might be driven into a corner, I will ask him for Madrī. So he took the form of a brāhman, came to the Bodisat, and said to him, "Give me as a slave this lovely sister, fair in all her limbs, unblamed by her husband, prized by her race." Then in anger spake Madrī to the brāhman, "O shameless and full of craving, do you long after her who is not lustful like you, O refuse of brāhmans, but takes her delight according to the upright law." Then the Bodisat Viśvantara began to look upon her with compassionate heart, and Madrī said to him, "I have no anxiety on my own account, I have no care for myself; my only anxiety is as to how you are to exist when remaining alone." Then said the Bodisat to Madrī, "As I seek after the height which surmounts endless anguish, no complaint must be uttered by me, O Madrī, upon this earth. Do you, therefore, follow after this brāhman without complaining. I will remain in the hermitage, living after the manner of the gazelles."

When he had uttered these words, he said to himself with joyous and exceedingly contented mind: This gift here in this forest is my best gift. After I have here absolutely given away Madrī, too, she shall by no means be recalled. Then he took Madrī by the hand and said to that brāhman, "Receive, O most excellent brāhman, this my dear wife, loving of heart, obedient to orders, charming in speech, demeaning herself as one of lofty race."

When, in order to attain to supreme insight, he had given away his beautiful wife, the earth quaked six times to its extremities like a boat on the water. And when Madrī had passed into the power of the brāhman, overcome by pain at being severed from her husband, her son, and her daughter, with faltering breath and in a voice which huskiness detained within her throat, she spoke thus, "What crime have I committed in my previous existence that now, like a cow whose calf is dead, I am lamenting in an uninhabited forest?" Then the king of the gods, Śakra, laid aside his brāhman's form, assumed his proper shape, and said to Madrī, "O fortunate one, I am not a brāhman nor am I a man at all. I am the king of the gods, Śakra, the subduer of the Asuras. As I am pleased that you have manifested the most excellent morality, say what desire you would now wish to have satisfied by me."

Rendered happy by these words, Madrī prostrated herself before Śakra, and said, "O thou of the thousand eyes, may the lord of the three and thirty set my children free from thralldom and let them find their way to their grandfather." After these words had been spoken the prince of the gods entered the hermitage and addressed the Bodisat. Taking Madrī by the left hand, he thus spake to the Bodisat, "I give you Madrī for your service. You must not give her to anyone. If you give away what has been entrusted to you, fault will be found with you."

Afterward the king of the gods, Śakra, deluded the brāhman who had carried off the boy and girl, so that under the impression that it was another city, he entered the selfsame city from which they had departed, and there set to work to sell the children. When the ministers saw this, they told the king, saying, "O king, your grandchildren, Krishṇa and Jālinī, have been brought into this good city in order to be sold, by an extremely worthless brāhman." When the king heard these words, he said indignantly, "Bring the children here, forthwith."

When this command had been attended to by the ministers, and the townspeople had hastened to appear before the king, one of the ministers brought the children before him. When the king saw his grandchildren brought before him, destitute of clothing and with foul bodies, he fell from his throne to the ground, and the assembly of ministers, and the women, and all who were present began to weep. Then the king said to the ministers, "Let the bright-eyed one, who, even when dwelling in the forest, delights in giving, be summoned hither at once, together with his wife."

After this the king of the gods, Śakra, having paid reverence to the Bodisat, returned to his own habitation.

Now, when King Viśvāmitra was dead, the brāhmans, the ministers, the townspeople, and the country people went to the hermitage and with entreaties invited the Bodisat to come to the city. There they installed him as king. Thereafter King Viśvantara was known by the name of Viśvatyāga (all-giver). And after he had made presents of various kinds to the sramaṇas, brāhmans, the poor and needy, his friends and relations, his acquaintances and servants, he uttered these ślokas: "In order to obtain supreme insight have I fearlessly bestowed gifts on kshatriyas, brāhmans, vaiśyas, sūdras, chandalas, and pukkasas, with gold and silver, oxen and horses, jeweled earrings, and laboring slaves. For giving is the most excellent of virtues. With a heart free from passion have I given away my wife and children, and obtained thereby power over men in this and the other world."

As King Viśvāmitra had, for Viśvantara's sake, bestowed great treasures on the brāhman Jujaka, who had thereby attained to great wealth, Jujaka's friends and relations, and those who were dear to him, came to him and said, "Your property and wealth and high fortune all depend upon Viśvantara." He replied, "What have I to do with Prince Viśvantara? As I was born in the first caste, I have obtained the recompense of the world, and therefore have I become so wealthy."

XXXIX

APHORISMS FROM THE TREE OF WISDOM

Buddhism in Tibet is so markedly different from varieties found elsewhere in Asia that it goes by a special name—Lamaism. It is a fusion of a late form of Indian Buddhism which entered Tibet in the Eighth Century A. D. with an original shamanistic nature worship of the land characterized by magic, sorcery and animism.

Tibetan literature reflects much of this mixed character of the religion. Yet it is not lacking in higher elements of knowledge drawn from earlier Buddhist teachings as these have been absorbed and passed on by the more capable and scholarly teachers. In addition to translations of works containing the classical doctrines of both Hīnayāna and Mahāyāna Buddhism, there is an ethical wisdom literature which appears in several collections of so-called "elegant sayings." These, though compiled by priests, are not so much expressions of religious doctrine as pithy observations on the conduct of life such as are found in the proverbs of many civilizations. The sayings quoted below are drawn from a work ascribed to Nāgārjuna, part of which was translated into Tibetan.[2]

> The root-principle of mankind is not to quarrel.
> What would you do with wealth obtained by quarreling?
> What would you do with wealth and life
> Obtained by pride and suppression of good?
>
> Whosoever does benefit to his enemy
> With straightforward intention,
> By so doing all enemies will arrive at
> The state of folding their hands in devotion.
>
> In desiring to injure your enemy
> Praise his inherent good qualities.
> What do evil thoughts of injury do?
> They injure you and not your enemy.
>
> Whenever the mean find a little wealth
> They despise everybody and are filled with pride;
> But the virtuous, although they may attain the
>   possession of wealth,
> Remain bowed like ripe rice.
>
> If they become possessed of wealth or learning
> Low people become proud.
> But even when doubly honored
> The wise man will become the more humble.
>
> Those blinded by desire do not perceive their sin.
> The blind man does not see the shape of [things];
> The proud do not perceive their faults.
> He who regards himself [the egotist] does not
>   perceive Real Truth.

[2] Selections of aphorisms from *She-Rab Dong-Bu,* tr. by W. L. Campbell. [Tree of Wisdom: (Tibetan) Śes-rab-Sdon-bu: (Sanskrit) Prajñā-Danda.]

If an astronomer calculates from the sky,
He will ascertain the paths of the moon and the stars:
But in his house the womenfolk are at variance,
And he does not perceive their various misconduct.

Even when young, rejoice in the intense tranquillity of the old.
Be not proud of what you know, even when learned.
However great your glory, be forbearing in your manner.
However high you may rise, be not proud.

Eating, sleeping, fearing and copulating—
Man and the brutes are alike in these.
By the practice of religion mankind is elevated.
If religion is not understood, is man not on a level with the brutes?

By compulsory separation excessive pain is infinitely caused to the mind.
But if the giving up is voluntary,
Infinite peaceful happiness will be obtained.

Whatever there be on the earth's surface—
Grain, gold, cattle, and good health,
Not all these will suffice to satisfy one man
If you understand this you will obtain tranquillity.

The great source of virtues, both visible and invisible, is knowledge.
Therefore, if you are striving to procure them,
Take hold of wisdom in its entirety.

Real Truth is a virtue to the talented,
But a harmful thing to those without talent.
The water of the river is very free from impurity;
But, entering the ocean, it becomes undrinkable.

The swan does not look well in an assemblage of hawks,
Nor the horse among the donkeys,
Nor the lion among the foxes,
Nor the clever man among fools.

Although a man may be learned in written works,
Yet if he does not apply [what he knows],
[He resembles] the blind man, who even with a
  lamp in his hand cannot see the road.

All desires should be abandoned,
But if you cannot abandon them,
Let your desire be for salvation.
That is the cure for it.

Whatever may be agreeable to your mind,
Although it be far away, is yet near.
That which is not kept firmly in mind,
Although by your side, is yet afar off.

Whoever gives alms which do not harm others—
His various [resulting] pleasures will neither be carried
  away by water,
Nor burned by fire, nor stolen by thieves.
Such possessions will never be utterly destroyed.

Let all hear this moral maxim,
And having heard it keep it well:
Whatever is not pleasing to yourself,
Do not that unto others.

The God of Death does not wait to ask whether
  your [composite] works are completed or not.
Therefore do tomorrow's work today,
And the evening's work in the morning.

If you desire ease, forsake learning.
If you desire learning, forsake ease.
How can the man at his ease acquire knowledge,
And how can the earnest student enjoy ease?

What country is foreign to a sage?
Who is hostile to a pleasant speaker?
What load is heavy to a man in his own home?
What distance is long to the energetic?

All the doings of fools are like ripples on water
    quickly effaced.
[The doings of] a holy man are like a carving on stone.
They may be small but they are permanent.

Intimacy in the society of the holy,
Conversation in the society of the learned,
And the friendship of the unselfish—
These will cause no regrets.

Although a thing may afford you mental enjoyment,
Yet, if the full fruition is to be injurious, how can it
    be right?
If anything upsets your health,
How can it be right to eat such a sweet dish?

That which hurts but is profitable
Is drunk by the wise like medicine.
The result, attained afterward,
Becomes in itself incomparable.

When the ocean shall be no more,
It may be crossed in the middle, so they say.
Whether holy men exist or not,
We should not transgress the moral codes.

APPENDIX

THE CEREMONY OF ORDINATION IN MODERN SIAM [1]

The ordination of a Buddhist monk is an impressive ceremony. Upon entering the Wat (or Monastery), accompanied by relatives and friends, the candidate finds himself before the Abbot, who is seated in front of the great image of the Buddha with his attendant monks grouped around him and all wearing the inscrutable and grave expression of reposeful meditation which is characteristic of the Order. The candidate seats himself upon the floor opposite the Abbot, while the congregation arranges itself, also sitting on the floor, on either side of him. Presents are then humbly offered by his relations to the monks, and a sponsor, leading him to the feet of the Abbot where he prostrates himself three times, presents him as a supplicant for admission to the Order. The Abbot thereupon solemnly catechizes the candidate as to his mental and bodily condition. The candidate, having made satisfactory replies to all questions, again prostrates himself with hands joined in the attitude of prayer and implores to be taken from the wicked world and received into the fold of the Order. Thereupon the name, age, and condition of the candidate are entered in a register, the robes and paraphernalia of a monk are brought forward, and the candidate is publicly stripped of the gala costume in which he has presented himself and is clothed by attendant monks in the holy yellow garments. The begging bowl is slung over his shoulder, the fan is placed in his hand, and thus habited he kneels once more before the Abbot and the sacred image towering behind him, and repeats so that all may hear:

> I go for refuge to the Buddha.
> I go for refuge to the Law.
> I go for refuge to the Order.

[1] Described by W. A. Graham, in his *Siam*, II, 232 ff.

Then, speaking after the Abbot, he takes upon himself the Ten Vows: to destroy no life of any kind; not to steal; to abstain from impurity; not to lie; to abstain from all intoxicants; not to eat at forbidden times; to abjure dancing, music, and all similar worldly delights; to use no scents or personal ornaments; to touch no gold, silver, or money; and to sleep only on the ground or on a low and narrow bed.

The Abbot then announces publicly that the candidate is received into the Order, and recites the list of duties which he must perform and of sins which he must avoid. Thereafter the parents, relatives, and friends of the newly ordained monk prostrate themselves in turn before him, at the same time offering him such small presents as he may receive without sinning, and having done this, leave him to take up his abode in the monastery where he must remain henceforth, or until he may ask to be relieved of his vows and to return to the world.

GLOSSARY [1]

Agni. Hindu fire-god; fire.
Ājīvaka sect. A community of ascetic mendicants, contemporary with the early Buddhists, whose asceticism included going without clothes; or, more shortly, one of the ascetic sects of Buddha's day.
Ālāra Kālāma. Gotama's earliest teacher in the art of meditation.
Amata. The deathless or the immortal state: a synonym for Nirvāṇa.
Ānanda. Gotama Buddha's cousin and personal attendant.
Anāthapiṇḍika. "Giver of alms to the unprotected": a name given to Sudatta, a lay patron of Buddha's order, famous for his gift of the monastery and grove called Jeta. (*See* Jeta.)
aññāsi. "He has attained (or perceived) the knowledge."
Aññātakondañña. "Kondañña who has attained (or perceived) the knowledge." Kondañña was the first of the five original disciples of Buddha.
Anuruddha. One of the Buddhist elders present at Buddha's death.
arahat (arhat). The perfected disciple or saint; one who has done everything required to reach the goal of his training.
ariya. Noble; the noble ones; hence, the elect.
āsavas (āsravas). Literally, "flowings," sometimes translated as "cankers"; specifically the āsavas are sensual desire, desire for becoming, and ignorance. To these is sometimes added wrong views.
āsītikapabba. "Having black joints." Name of a plant. *See also* kālāpabba.
Assaji. One of the five original disciples of Buddha.
Bhaddiya. One of the five original disciples of Buddha.
bhikku (bhikshu). A Buddhist monk; a mendicant.

[1] Sanskrit equivalents of Pāli words are in parentheses.

Bhoganagara. A place northward of Vesāli, visited by Buddha on his journeys.

bīrana. A kind of weed-grass which infests rice fields.

bodhisat (bodhisattva). One striving earnestly for enlightenment to fit himself to aid his fellow men.

Brahmā. One of the great gods, in Buddhism conceived as a personal being.

brāhman, or *brāhmin.* A member of the Hindu priestly caste.

brāhmana. Same as brāhman; also used to denote an ideal holy man or true saint, as in *Dhammapada,* Ch. XXVI.

Brahman. The Supreme Being; Supreme Reality.

Buddha. The Enlightened One.

cankers. See *āsavas.*

Channa. One of Buddha's monks.

chāpa. An ordinary bow.

Chunda. The metal worker who served Buddha his last meal.

deva. A god or deity of Hindu mythology; a shining or heavenly one.

Dhamma (Dharma). Doctrine, Law or Teaching of Buddha; more generally, any system, set of doctrines and duties, way of life.

Dhanapālaka. "Guardian of wealth": name of an elephant.

dhāranī. Spells; words or sentences having magic power.

Dukkha. Ill; Suffering; Pain; Woe; Misery. The first of the Four Noble Truths.

Eightfold Path. See Editor's Introduction, p. xvi.

Ens and non-Ens. Being and non-Being.

Four Noble Truths. Suffering, its cause, its cessation, and the path leading to its cessation.

Four Signs. Old age, sickness, death, and a recluse—the four sights which led Gotama to renounce the world.

Gandharva. A demigod; one of the heavenly musicians.

gāthā. Verses; poem composed of verses.

Gayāsīsa. Gayā-Head, a hill overlooking the town of Gayā.

ghât. In India, a landing place, with stairs descending to a river for purposes of bathing, etc.

Ill. See *Dukkha.*

GLOSSARY

Indra (or Śakra). The king of the gods.

Isipatana. The deer-park at Benares.

Jeta. A prince after whom the grove of Jeta with its famous monastery (Jetavana) was named.

kālāpabba. "Having black joints." Name of a plant. *See also* āsītikapabba.

karavīra. Oleander.

karma. Retribution of actions; the law of ethical consequence.

Kāsis. Name of a tribe whose chief city was Benares on the Ganges.

khandas. The five physical and mental elements constituting an individual. These are rūpa (body), vedanā (sensation), saññā (perception), the aggregates (sankhārā), and consciousness (viññāṇa).

kodanda. A cross-bow.

Kondañña. The first of the first five disciples of Buddha.

kshatriya. A warrior; member of the warrior caste.

Kusinārā. A place in the country of the Mallas (a tribe) where Buddha passed away.

Magadhas. People of the Kingdom of Magadha.

Maghavan. Lord of bounty; the generous one. An epithet of Indra.

Mahānāma. One of the five original disciples of Buddha.

Mahāvagga. "Great Series." A collection of books in the canonical literature having to do with the organization of the Order.

Mallikā. Jasmine.

Mālunkyā-pūtta. "Son of Mālunkyā": name of an ascetic.

Māra. Lord of the realm of sense; the Evil One; the Tempter.

Moggallāna. One of Buddha's two chief disciples.

Muni. A sage. As title of Buddha, Sakyamuni means Sage of the Sakya [tribe].

Name-and-form (nāma-rūpa). Mind and body.

Nerāñjarā. The river near which Gotama became enlightened.

Nibbāna (Nirvāṇa). The state of transcendent attainment; release from the limitations of existence and from rebirth; the ultimate goal.

pabbajā. The ceremony of leaving the world to become a Buddhist monk.

paribbājaka. A wandering mendicant.
Pāvā. The chief town of the clan known as the Mallas.
Petas (Pretas). Ghosts; "departed ones," who dwell in a realm where they are tortured by hunger and thirst.
rāja. A king or ruler.
Rājagaha. Capital city of the tribe called Magadhas.
rānee. Wife of a rāja.
rishi. A sage.
rūpa. Body, bodily form. One of the five physical and mental constituents of the individual. *See* khandas.
Sakyan. Member of the Sakya tribe.
samādhi. Concentrated state of mind; trance.
sambodhi. Complete enlightenment.
samana (śramana). An ascetic.
sammāsambbuddho. Supreme, perfectly enlightened one.
Saṃsāra. Transmigration; the world of change in which transmigration takes place; the realm of transmigratory existence.
Sangha. The Order of monks.
Sañjaya. An ascetic and teacher of Sāriputta and Moggalāna before they became followers of Buddha.
sankhārā (saṃskāra). Aggregates; one of the groups of mental constituents in the five-fold division of the individual. *See* khandas.
saññā. Perception: one of the five groups constituting the individual. *See* khandas.
Sāriputta. One of Buddha's two chief disciples.
Sāti. The fisherman's son whom Buddha instructed on the nature of consciousness.
Sāvatthi. The capital of the kingdom of Kosala, located near the Himalaya mountains within what is now Nepal.
sotāpatti (śrotāpatti). "Entering the stream"; entrance upon the Buddhist way of life; the first step on the holy way.
śramana. See *samana.*
śrāvaka. A disciple.
Sugata. "He who has well gone"; a title of Buddha, who has gone to Nirvāna.
Śūnya. The Void; the Emptiness of all relative existence.
synergies. See sankhāras.

Tathāgata. "Thus come" or "thus gone"; i.e. he who has come (or gone) as have the former Buddhas; he who has arrived at Truth; the Truth-finder. A title of Gotama Buddha.

Uddaka Rāmaputta. One of the two teachers of Gotama in the art of meditation.

Upaka. An ascetic belonging to the Ājīvaka Sect who questioned Buddha concerning his enlightenment.

upasampadā. The ceremony of ordination as a Buddhist monk.

urdhvamsrotas. "One who swims against the stream and is not carried away by the vulgar passions of the world."—Max Müller.

Uruvelā. One of the minor towns in the land of the Magadhas, situated on the bank of the river Nerāñjarā, where Gotama attained enlightenment.

Vappa. One of Buddha's first five disciples.

Vassikī. Name of a flower.

vedanā. Sensation of feeling: one of the five constituents of the individual. *See* khandas.

viññana. Consciousness: one of the five constituents of the individual. *See* khandas.

Yama. The first human being to die; ruler of the realm of the departed; personification of death.

BIBLIOGRAPHY

Sources for Selections in This Book

Anesaki, Masaharu. *Nichiren the Buddhist Prophet.* Cambridge: Harvard University Press, 1916.
Buddhist Parables. Tr. from the original Pāli by Eugene Watson Burlingame. New Haven: Yale University Press, 1922.
Buddhist Scriptures. A selection. Tr. from the Pāli, with an introduction, by E. J. Thomas. London: John Murray, 1913.
Dhammapada. A collection of verses; being one of the canonical books of the Buddhists. Tr. from the Pāli by F. Max Müller. ("The Sacred Books of the East," Vol. X.) Oxford: The Clarendon Press, 1881.
Graham, W. A., *Siam.* 2 v. London: Alexander Moring, Ltd., 1924.
Jatakas, Nidāna-kathā. Buddhist birth stories (Jataka tales); the commentarial introduction entitled Nidāna-kathā, the story of the lineage. Tr. by T. W. Rhys Davids. New and rev. ed. by Mrs. Rhys Davids. New York: E. P. Dutton & Co., 1925.
Kanjur. Tibetan Tales, Derived from Indian Sources. Tr. from the Tibetan into German by F. Anton von Schiefner, and from the German by W. R. S. Ralston. New Edition by C. A. F. Rhys Davids. New York: Dutton & Co., 1926.
K'uei Chi. *Wei-shih-er-shih-lun Shu-chi* (in Chinese). Kiangsi, China: Buddhist Publishing House, 1909. 2 vols.
Lee, Shao Chang. *Popular Buddhism in China.* Shanghai: Commercial Press, Ltd., 1939.
The Life of Gotama the Buddha. Compiled exclusively from the Pāli Canon by E. H. Brewster. New York: E. P. Dutton & Co., 1926.
Mahāvastu [The Great Story]. Tr. from the Buddhist Sanskrit by J. J. Jones. ("Sacred Books of the Buddhists," Vol. XVI) London: Luzac & Co., Ltd., 1949.
Majjhima Nikāya. Further Dialogues of the Buddha. Tr. by Lord [Sir Robert] Chalmers from the Pāli of the Majjhima Nikāya, or Discourses of Medium Length. ("Sacred Books of the Bud-

dhists," Vols. V and VI.) 2 vols. London: Luzac & Co., Ltd., 1926-27.

Nāgārjuna (Lu-Trub). *The Tree of Wisdom*. Tr. by Major W. L. Campbell from the Tibetan version (She-Rab Dong-Bu) of the Sanskrit original (Prajnya Danda). Calcutta: Published by the Calcutta University at the Baptist Mission Press, 1919.

Reichelt, Karl Ludvig. *Truth and Tradition in Chinese Buddhism*. Tr. from the Norwegian by Kathrina van Wagenen Bugge. Shanghai: The Commercial Press, Ltd., 1927.

The Road to Nirvana. A selection of the Buddhist Scriptures. Tr. from the Pāli by E. J. Thomas. ("The Wisdom of the East Series.") London: John Murray, 1950.

Saddharmapuṇḍarika. The Lotus of the Wonderful Law, or the Miao-fa lien-hua ching. Tr. from the Chinese by W. E. Soothill. Oxford: The Clarendon Press, 1930.

Shinran. *Buddhist Psalms*. Tr. by S. Yamabe and L. Adams Beck. ("The Wisdom of the East Series.") New York: Dutton & Co., 1921.

Shunjō. *Honen the Buddhist Saint: His Life and Teaching*. Compiled by imperial order. Translation, historical introduction, explanatory and critical notes by Rev. Harper Havelock Coates and Rev. Ryugaku Ishizuka. Kyoto: Chionin, 1925.

Smith, Vincent A. *Asoka, the Buddhist Emperor of India*. 2nd ed. Oxford: Clarendon Press, 1909.

Stcherbatsky, T. I. *The Conception of Buddhist Nirvāṇa* (with translation of Chs. I and XXV of Chandrakīrti's *Prasaññapadā*). Leningrad, 1927. Shanghai Reprint, 1940.

Suttanipāta. Buddha's Teachings. Being the Sutta-nipāta, or Discourse-collection. Edited in the original Pāli text, with an English version facing it, by Lord [Sir Robert] Chalmers. ("Harvard Oriental Series," Vol. XXXVII) Cambridge, Mass: Harvard University Press.

Suzuki, Daisetz Teitaro. *Manual of Zen Buddhism*. Kyoto: The Eastern Buddhist Society, 1935.

Thomas, Edward J. *The Life of Buddha as Legend and History*. New York: Alfred A. Knopf, 1927.

Vasubandhu. *The Treatise in Twenty Stanzas on Representation-Only*. Tr. by Clarence H. Hamilton from Wei Shih Er Shih Luṇ

the Chinese version of the original Sanskrit Vijñaptimātratā-siddhi; Viṃśatika. New Haven, Conn.: American Oriental Society, 1938.
"Vimalakīrti-nirdeśa Sūtra," *The Eastern Buddhist,* Vol. III, No. 2 (July-August-September), 1924. Tr. by Hokei Idumi.

Books for Further Reading

Armstrong, Robert Cornell. *Buddhism and Buddhists in Japan.* New York: The Macmillan Company, 1927.
Aṣvaghosha. *The Fo-sho-hing-tsan-king.* A life of Buddha, translated from Sanskrit into Chinese by Dharmaraksha, 420 A.D., and from Chinese into English by Samuel Beal. ("The Sacred Books of the East," Vol. XIX.) Oxford: The Clarendon Press, 1883.
Bacot, Jacques. *Le Bouddha.* ("Mythes et religions," Vol. XX.) Paris: Presses universitaires de France, 1947.
Buddhism in Translations. Passages selected from the Pāli Canon and translated into English by Henry Clarke Warren. ("Harvard Oriental Series," Vol. III.) Cambridge, Mass.: Harvard University Press, 8th printing, 1922.
Coomaraswamy, Ananda. *Hinduism and Buddhism.* New York: Philosophical Library.
Davids, Mrs. Caroline Augusta (Foley) Rhys. *Buddhism,* a study of the Buddhist Norm. ("Home University Library of Modern Knowledge," No. 44). New York: H. Holt and Company, 1912.
———. *Gotama the Man.* London: Luzac & Co., 1928.
———. *A Manual of Buddhism for Advanced Students.* New York: The Macmillan Co., 1932.
Dayal, Har. *The Bodhisattva Doctrine in Buddhist Sanskrit Literature.* London: K. Paul, Trench, Trubner & Co., Ltd., 1932.
Dhammapada. The Buddha's Way of Virtue. Tr. from the Pāli by W. D. C. Wagiswara and K. J. Saunders. ("The Wisdom of the East Series.") London: John Murray, 1912.
Eliot, Sir Charles Norton Edgecumbe. *Hinduism and Buddhism.* An Historical Sketch. London: E. Arnold & Co., 1921. 3 vols.
———. *Japanese Buddhism.* London: E. Arnold & Co., 1935.

Goddard, Dwight. *A Buddhist Bible.* 2nd ed. rev. and enl. Edited and published by Dwight Goddard. Thetford, Vt., 1938.

Grousset, René. *In the Footsteps of the Buddha.* Tr. from the French by Mariette Léon. London: George Routledge & Sons, 1932.

Hackmann, Heinrich. *Buddhism as a Religion.* Its Historical Development and Its Present Conditions. From the German, revised and enlarged by the author. ("Probsthain's Oriental Series," Vol. II.) London: Probsthain, 1910.

Hamilton, Clarence Herbert. *Buddhism in India, Ceylon, China and Japan.* A Reading Guide. Chicago, Ill.: University of Chicago Press, 1931.

Heiler, Friedrich. *Die Buddhistische Versenkung.* Eine religionsgeschichtliche Untersuchung. München: E. Reinhardt, 1922.

Horner, I. *Women Under Primitive Buddhism.* Laywomen and almswomen. ("The Broadway Oriental Library.") London: G. Routledge & Sons, Ltd., 1930.

Johnson, Sir Reginald. *Buddhist China.* Ill. New York: Dutton, 1913.

Keith, Arthur Berriedale. *Buddhist Philosophy in India and Ceylon.* Oxford: The Clarendon Press, 1923.

Kern, Hendrick. *Manual of Indian Buddhism.* Strassburg: K. J. Trubner, 1896.

La Vallée Poussin, Louis de. *Bouddhisme.* Opinions sur l'histoire de la dogmatique. 3d ed. Paris: G. Beauchesne, 1925.

———. *The Way to Nirvāṇa:* Six lectures on Ancient Buddhism as a Discipline of Salvation. Cambridge (Engl.): The University Press, 1917.

———. *Le dogme et la philosophie du Bouddhisme.* ("Études sur l'histoire des religions," VI.) Paris: Gabriel Beauchesne, 1930.

Oldenberg, Hermann. *Buddha: His Life, His Doctrine, His Order.* Tr. from the German by William Hoey. London, Edinburgh: Williams and Norgate, 1882.

Pratt, James Bissett. *The Pilgrimage of Buddhism and a Buddhist Pilgrimage.* New York: The Macmillan Company, 1928.

The Quest of Enlightenment. A selection of the Buddhist Scriptures, translated from the Sanskrit by E. J. Thomas. ("The Wisdom of the East Series.") London: John Murray, 1950.

Śānti-deva. *The Path of Light.* A Manual of Mahāyāna Buddhism. Tr. by L. D. Barnett from Bodhicharyāvatāra. ("The Wisdom of the East Series") London: John Murray. 2nd edition, 1947.

Saunders, Kenneth J. *Gotama Buddha.* A biography based on the canonical books of the Theravādin. New York: Association Press, 1920.

———. *Buddhism and Buddhists in Southern Asia.* New York: The Macmillan Company, 1923.

———. *Epochs in Buddhist History.* ("The Haskell Lectures in Comparative Religion") Chicago: The University of Chicago Press, 1924.

Schayer, Stanislav. *Mahāyāna Doctrines of Salvation.* Tr. from the German by R. T. Knight. London: Probsthain & Co., 1923.

Steinilber-Oberlin, Emile. *The Buddhist Sects of Japan, their history, philosophical doctrines and sanctuaries.* Tr. from the French by Marc Logé. London: G. Allen & Unwin, Ltd., 1938.

Suzuki, Beatrice (Lane). *Mahāyāna Buddhism.* With an Introduction by D. T. Suzuki and a Foreword by Christmas Humphreys. 2nd ed. enl. London: D. Marlowe, 1948.

Suzuki, Daisetz Teitaro. *Essays in Zen Buddhism.* (First Series.) London: Luzac and Company, 1927.

Takakusu, Junjiro. *The Essentials of Buddhist Philosophy.* Honolulu: University of Hawaii, 1947, 1949.

Thomas, Edward J. *The History of Buddhist Thought.* New York: Alfred A. Knopf, 1933.

Waddell, Laurence Austine. *The Buddhism of Tibet:* or Lamaism, with its mystic cults, symbolism and mythology, and in its relation to Indian Buddhism. 2nd ed. Cambridge, Eng.: W. Heffer & Sons, Ltd., 1939.

Winternitz, Moriz. *Geschichte der indischen Literatur.* ("Die buddhistische Literatur und die heiligen Texte der Jainas." Vol II.) Leipzig: C. F. Amelang, 1920.

———. *A History of Indian Literature,* Buddhist Literature and Jaina Literature. Vol. II. Tr. from the German by Mrs. S. Ketkar and Miss H. Kohn, and revised by the author. Calcutta: University of Calcutta, 1933.

———. *Der Mahāyāna-buddhismus, nach sanskrit und prakrit Texten.* Tübingen: Mohr, 1930.

 The Library of Liberal Arts

AESCHYLUS, Prometheus Bound
D'ALEMBERT, J., Preliminary
    Discourse to the
    Encyclopedia of Diderot
AQUINAS, ST. T., The Principles of
    Nature, On Being and
    Essence, On Free Choice,
    and On the Virtues in
    General
ARISTOTLE, Nicomachean Ethics
    On Poetry and Music
    On Poetry and Style
ARNAULD, A., The Art of Thinking
    (Port-Royal Logic)
AUGUSTINE, ST., On Christian
    Doctrine
    On Free Choice of the Will
BACON, F., The New Organon
BARON and BLAU, eds., Judaism
BAUDELAIRE, C., The Prophetic
    Muse: Critical Essays of
    Baudelaire
BAYLE, P., Historical and Critical
    Dictionary (Selections)
BECCARIA, C., On Crimes and
    Punishments
BERGSON, H., Duration and
    Simultaneity
    Introduction to Metaphysics
BERKELEY, G., Principles,
    Dialogues, *and*
    Philosophical
    Correspondence

Principles of
    Human Knowledge
Three Dialogues Between
    Hylas and Philonous
Works on Vision
BOCCACCIO, G., On Poetry
BOETHIUS, The Consolation of
    Philosophy
BOILEAU, N., Selected Criticism
BOLINGBROKE, H., The Idea of a
    Patriot King
BONAVENTURA, ST., The Mind's
    Road to God
BOSANQUET, B., Three Lectures on
    Aesthetic
BOWMAN, A., The Absurdity of
    Christianity
BRADLEY, F., Ethical Studies
BURKE, E., An Appeal from the
    New to the Old Whigs
    Reflections on the Revolution
    in France
    Selected Writings and
    Speeches on America
BURKE, K., Permanence and
    Change
BUTLER, J., Five Sermons
CALVIN, J., On the Christian Faith
    On God and Political Duty
CATULLUS, Odi et Amo:
    Complete Poetry
CICERO, On the Commonwealth
Cid, The Epic of the

CROCE, B., Guide to Aesthetics
DESCARTES, R., Discourse on Method
   Discourse on Method *and* Meditations
   Discourse on Method, Optics, Geometry, *and* Meteorology
   Meditations
   Philosophical Essays
   Rules for the Direction of the Mind
DEWEY, J., On Experience, Nature, and Freedom
DIDEROT, D., Encyclopedia (Selections)
   Rameau's Nephew and Other Works
DOSTOEVSKI, F., The Grand Inquisitor
DRYDEN, J., An Essay of Dramatic Poesy and Other Essays
DUNS SCOTUS, J., Philosophical Writings
EPICTETUS, The Enchiridion
EPICURUS, Letters, Principal Doctrines, *and* Vatican Sayings
ERASMUS, D., Ten Colloquies
EURIPIDES, Electra
FEUERBACH, L., Principles of the Philosophy of the Future
FICHTE, J., The Vocation of Man
GOETHE, J., Faust I and II (verse)
   Faust I (prose)
   Faust II (prose)
GRANT, F., ed., Ancient Roman Religion
   Hellenistic Religions
GRIMMELSHAUSEN, J., Simplicius Simplicissimus
GROTIUS, H., Prolegomena to The Law of War and Peace

HAMILTON, C., ed., Buddhism
HANSLICK, E., The Beautiful in Music
HENDEL, C., Jean-Jacques Rousseau: Moralist
   Studies in the Philosophy of David Hume
HERDER, J., God, Some Conversations
HESIOD, Theogony
HOBBES, T., Leviathan I and II
HORACE, The Odes of Horace *and* The Centennial Hymn
HUME, D., Dialogues Concerning Natural Religion
   Inquiry Concerning Human Understanding
   Inquiry Concerning the Principles of Morals
   Of the Standard of Taste, and Other Essays
   Philosophical Historian
   Political Essays
JEFFERY, A., ed., Islam
KANT, I., Analytic of the Beautiful
   Critique of Practical Reason
   First Introduction to the Critique of Judgment
   Foundations of the Metaphysics of Morals
   The Metaphysical Elements of Justice, Part I of *Metaphysik der Sitten*
   The Metaphysical Principles of Virtue, Part II of *Metaphysik der Sitten*
   On History
   Perpetual Peace
   Prolegomena to Any Future Metaphysics
KLEIST, H., The Prince of Homburg
LAO TZU, The Way of Lao Tzu
Lazarillo de Tormes, The Life of

LEIBNIZ, G., Monadology and Other Philosophical Essays
LESSING, G., Laocoön
LOCKE, J., A Letter Concerning Toleration
Second Treatise of Government
LONGINUS, On Great Writing (On the Sublime)
LUCIAN, Selected Works
LUCRETIUS, On Nature
MACHIAVELLI, N., The Art of War
Mandragola
MARCUS AURELIUS, Meditations
MEAD, G., Selected Writings
MILL, J., An Essay on Government
MILL, J. S., Autobiography
Considerations on Representative Government
Nature *and* Utility of Religion
On Liberty
On the Logic of the Moral Sciences
Theism
Utilitarianism
MOLIÈRE, Tartuffe
MONTESQUIEU, C., The Persian Letters
NIETZSCHE, F., The Use and Abuse of History
NOVALIS, Hymns to the Night and Other Writings
OCKHAM, W., Philosophical Writings
PAINE, T., The Age of Reason
PALEY, W., Natural Theology
PARKINSON, T., ed., Masterworks of Prose
PICO DELLA MIRANDOLA, On the Dignity of Man, On Being and the One, *and* Heptaplus

PLATO, Epistles
Euthydemus
Euthyphro, Apology, Crito
Gorgias
Meno
Phaedo
Phaedrus
Protagoras
Statesman
Symposium
Theaetetus
Timaeus
Commentaries:
BLUCK, R., Plato's Phaedo
CORNFORD, F., Plato and Parmenides
Plato's Cosmology
Plato's Theory of Knowledge
HACKFORTH, R., Plato's Examination of Pleasure
Plato's Phaedo
Plato's Phaedrus
PLAUTUS, The Haunted House
The Menaechmi
The Rope
POPE, A., An Essay on Man
POST, C., ed., Significant Cases in British Constitutional Law
QUINTILIAN, On the Early Education of the Citizen-Orator
REYNOLDS, J., Discourses on Art
Roman Drama, Copley and Hadas, trans.
ROSENMEYER, OSTWALD, and HALPORN, The Meters of Greek and Latin Poetry
RUSSELL, B., Philosophy of Science
Sappho, The Poems of

SCHILLER, J., Wilhelm Tell
SCHLEGEL, J., On Imitation and Other Essays
SCHNEIDER, H., Sources of Contemporary Philosophical Realism in America
SCHOPENHAUER, A., On the Basis of Morality
    Freedom of the Will
SELBY-BIGGE, L., British Moralists
SENECA, Medea
    Oedipus
    Thyestes
SHAFTESBURY, A., Characteristics
SHELLEY, P., A Defence of Poetry
SMITH, A., The Wealth of Nations (Selections)
Song of Roland, Terry, trans.
SOPHOCLES, Electra
SPIEGELBERG, H., The Socratic Enigma

SPINOZA, B., Earlier Philosophical Writings
    On the Improvement of the Understanding
TERENCE, The Brothers
    The Eunuch
    The Mother-in-Law
    Phormio
    The Self-Tormentor
    The Woman of Andros
Three Greek Romances, Hadas, trans.
TOLSTOY, L., What is Art?
VERGIL, Aeneid
VICO, G. B., On the Study Methods Our Time
VOLTAIRE, Philosophical Letters
WHITEHEAD, A., Interpretation of Science
WOLFF, C., Preliminary Discourse on Philosophy in General
XENOPHON, Recollections of Socrates *and* Socrates' Defense Before the Jury

"Middle Path" p. 28

· Poem re death of Buddha p. 46

Cf. verse akin to Daoism p. 76
        immortality v Nirvana (?) p 66

Cf. the self as responsible for oneself ..(78), he who fails to dev.
         discipline (77)

Cf. drink. p 84 → is it a passion/desire
                    c a pleasure of life p. 95?
                    "sensual pleasures" p. 108.

· % Perfect wisdom one ferries to the Other Shore 113-15
                                v the Void

★ Hui-yuan's 'White Lotus Ode' (124f.)
    ↪ Lindo (?)/Honan on Amida's 'Original Vow' (140)

Case of Vimalakirti, Buddhist living w/in the world, 146 ff